HIS

HIS

By

Marilyn Majors

Golden Horizons Publishing

ISBN: 979-8-9928246-1-2 (paperback)
ISBN: 979-8-9928246-2-9 (hardcover)
ISBN: 979-8-9928246-3-6 (eBook)

GHP

GOLDEN HORIZONS
PUBLISHING

Table of Contents

Special Acknowledgement

🦋 To the One who has carried me so far, I would like to give the first fruits of my praise. To the One who has never left my side and never backed away from my emotions. The One who allowed me to take the long way around and always made me first even during the times that I put Him last. Abba, Father, from the deepest part of my heart I thank You. I pray that this book gives You all the honor and all the glory and strengthens Your daughters as they walk with You.

🦋 To my mom, HIS is dedicated to the memory of you. How I wish I had taken every opportunity granted to me to get to know you better, spend more time with you and just be by your side. Without your help mom, I wouldn't be where I'm at today and I am forever grateful.

🦋 To my son, my number one always, this book is dedicated to you. God filled my cup to overflowing when He allowed me to be your mother. The amount of joy and happiness you continue to bring me is endless. My desire always is that you stay close to God and know your value and calling in Him. He has big plans for you son, and I pray He continues to lead you. Side note: We've got to get back to the beach soon. (hugs)

🦋 To my sister, Loren Davidson, where do I even begin? Though we have been a part of each other's lives for about 4 years now, it feels as though we have always known each other. I am so grateful for all the experiences we have been through together and how our bond just continues to grow. The love of Christ shines within you and you radiate His beauty. Don't ever stop praising Him.

🦋 To Ambria Harmon (another bond that happened so quickly), thank you for always being there for me, believing in, and supporting me sis. There is no doubt in my mind that God has so much in store for you and I am here to cheer you on every step of the way. You are so incredibly smart and talented, and I can't wait to see what life has in store for you. You're totally the bees knees.

🦋 To my brother, Curtis Majors, you are the strongest and most selfless man that I know. It is such an honor to be your little sister. Thank you for showing up every time I had a problem that I didn't know how to solve. Despite what's going on your way, you always make time for me. For that, I am grateful. You are amazing and one of a kind. I love you.

🦋 To Ashley Murrell, what an honor and a privilege it is to be working with you once again. Thank you for making this a smooth and fun process as well as a praying one. Thank you for all your encouragement and feedback. I cannot thank you enough for taking a chance on me.

🦋 To Rosetta Milburn, you always said I should write a book. By the grace of God, here we are.

🦋 To Rose and Katie Graham, I have seen life throw so much your way and you keep standing and rising. You are both the most resilient and strong ladies that I know. Also, you two are such an inspiration to me and all who are blessed to be in your presence.

🦋 To all those who knew about this book before the first poem/word was type, thank you. Thank you for being the type of friends and sisters that I can share and trust my life with. Thank you all for praying for me and for this book. Thank you for the excitement and support shown while on this journey. It was the fuel that kept me going/writing.

(Please forgive me if I fail to mention by name) Thank you to Casey Ruckle, Heather Smith Gordon, Paige Danielle, and Collen Webber. Thank you all for cheering me on. I pray that HIS blesses you.

Without further ado, I introduce you to **HIS.**

Introduction

STRIP AWAY

Strip away your job title. Strip away your name. Strip away the many hats you wear as mom, daughter, sister, friend, neighbor, etc. Strip away your educational and generational background. What's left standing? Who are you at the core? If we were to strip away all the information that the world uses to identify you, what or rather who would you be?

IDENTITY

From the moment you're born, the world begins to identify you. Your parents are given your birth certificate that identifies and lets others know your name, race, gender. As we grow, we are identified by our hobbies, our talents, even our looks. In high school, it's all about the college we plan to attend or our goals for the future. We live in a world that tells us to find our identity/ourselves within our careers, within relationships, what we have collected, and what makes us happy. **IDENTITY**. Such a heavy, loaded word. God has been working with me personally on my identity. And it is an honor and a privilege to pour out onto these pages what He has poured into me (please note: I am still and will continue to be a work in progress until He calls me to glory). When we know who we are in Christ, everything around us changes. How we view situations changes. How we respond to people changes. Who we are at the inner core changes as

He allows us just a glimpse of how He sees us. Why go back to the worldly view and definition on things when God has walked you through the spiritual? I spent a big part of my life chasing my identity, but I didn't know it. For a season of my life, I went from job to job (some places I would only stay a few months at and some I would just walk out and leave…which definitely wasn't the way to handle things) unsatisfied and immediately would look for the next thing. For a part of the season, if I wasn't getting attention from the opposite sex, I would be convinced that there was something wrong with me. (God has shown me that honesty and transparency is vital in healing as well as accountability, so I will gladly tell on myself…more so when it points the way back to Him). Me not knowing my identity as well as worth/value in Christ is what had me chasing all the wrong things. I was seeking validation from a society that is always changing, was looking for completion from those who were carrying their own baggage but weren't ready to release and deal with it.

Growing up, I could tell you my name, street address, who my parents were, and where I went to school. However, I couldn't tell you about the girl staring back at me in the mirror. God met me in the middle of my mess, took me by the hand, and started to allow me to see myself as He sees me. The journey was messy. It was painful yet purposeful. I was stubborn at times by refusing to believe that the Creator of the whole world still loved me flaws and all.

When you know your identity in Christ, the enemy's lies fall to the floor. When you know your identity in Christ, you won't walk where most people are walking because you've locked eyes with Him and He is leading the way. When you know your identity in Christ, the authority and anointing from the throne room of heaven falls down upon you sis. So, remember who you are in Him.

PURPOSE

HIS is a gentle but firm reminder of who we are in Christ, what we are called to do, and truly exploring our identity and value in Him. We never intended to look to the world for our identity, because it has taken the broad path. Our culture is constantly redefining and changing identity. We were never intended to seek value and validation from people, but we were created to sit at our Saviors feet and look to Him for everything that we need. Don't you know that you are an image bearer of Christ (*Genesis 1:26 KJV*), called to be set apart (*Psalm 4:3*), and chosen by Him (*1st Peter 2:9*)? Don't you know that you are the apple of His eye *(Psalm 17:8)*, the one He delights in (*Zephaniah 3:17*), and as long as you seek Him, He will lead you beside still waters (*Psalm 23:2b*)?

So, put the phone down for a little while sis. Turn off the TV and close social media (it will still be there I promise). Inhale, exhale and let go of the worries, the stress, and the responsibilities from your day. Grab a cup of tea as well as your favorite blanket and ask God to meet you here in this moment as you go from page to page. Nothing ever happens by chance, and I am so glad that this book has found its way to you. I pray that this book opens up your eyes to who you are in Him and stirs up within you a renewed hunger and thirst for Him. I pray that within these pages, comfort is found, joy is rediscovered, peace restored, but more than anything, I pray that **HIS** is a reminder of who you are and whose you are. (*1st Peter 2:9*)

Before you dive in, may I pray with you?

Abba Father,

I thank You Lord for the person that is holding this book. I pray Father God that they will hear your still small voice within these pages. Lord, I pray that the words upon these pages touches them, heals them, and allows them to let go of anything that has been a hinderance in their walk with you Lord. Father God, please strengthen them where they are weak. Revive them where they are weary. Hold them dear Lord when they feel as though they are falling apart. May Your peace, may Your presence, and may Your joy be a covering over them.

In Yeshua's name I pray,

Amen.

You are **HIS** sis. Simply, beautifully **HIS**.

Poems

No Longer

No longer guilty
I've been set free
By the One whose blood
Righteously redeems

No longer ashamed
Of the girl I used to be
Cause I've fallen in love with my Jesus
And He is doing something new within me

No longer shackled
And bound to my past
For He's spoken over me
And His words shall last

No longer fearful
Of what tomorrow may hold
Cause I am held by my Savior
He has touched my soul

No longer worried about
How I am perceived by this world
Cause I have found my identity
In the One who says that I am His girl

No longer coming into agreement
With fear, worry, and doubt.
I've placed my trust in Yeshua
And He has it all figured out

No longer compromising
Or settling for hurt
Cause my Jesus has opened up my eyes
To allow me to see my worth

No longer apart of this world
Oh, how I long to do my Father's will
To be led beside peaceful waters
As He whispers to my soul "be still"

No longer disappointed
When things don't go my way and people leave
Cause with my Jesus, I am never forsaken
I am never empty

No longer listening to the voice
That tells me everything that I "can't" do
Cause when I read the word of God
I know that this is not true

No longer trying to live up
To who or what they think I ought to be
I listen to my Shephard
Cause I am His sheep

No longer wandering in Egypt
I've left it all behind
I'm picking up my cross daily
And following after this Savior of mine.

Ever Since

Ever since You called my name
Ever since You pulled me out of the dark
Oh; how I've been changed
And given a new heart

Ever since I was little
Ever since I started to grow
You had Your eyes on me
Looking out for my soul

Ever since the world was created
Ever since the beginning of time
You set me apart for a greater purpose
And whispered "she is Mine"

Ever since I read Your promises
Ever since I've believed that they are true
You've shown me that nothing is impossible
As long as I walk with You

Ever since You touched my hand,
Ever since You touched my soul
Of the worlds lies and ways
I'm letting go

Ever since You found me in the wilderness
Ever since You allowed me to see

You truly are the only one
That can fill me when I'm empty

Ever since You stepped into my life
Ever since You called me Your own
I've been changed from the inside out
As it's now, Holy Spirit's home

Ever since You called me out of Egypt
Ever since You showed me that You are the truth
and the way
Lord, I just want to pick up my cross daily
And in Your presence
I long to stay.

(Until) You Became

I was lost in the dark
Until You became my light
I was living life all wrong
Until You became my right

I was blind
Until You gave me eyes to see
Just how amazing You are
And how much You care for me

I was hopeless
Until You became my hope
I was an emotional wreck
Until You taught me how to cope

I was a sheep aimlessly wandering
Until You became my Shephard
I was running on empty
Until You became my helper

I was holding on to things
That were slipping through my hands
Leaning on my own ways
Until You gave me
Wisdom to understand

That I was created for a purpose
I was created by You
To be a sold-out vessel
Cause there's much work to do

I was drinking from the cup of compromise
Until You became my source of living waters
I wore the titles that the world gave me
Until I became Your daughter

Cause I felt invisible
Until You became El-Roi
The God who sees
And now, no longer will I let another define me

You see, I was lost in my sin
Until You became my Redeemer
I was a prisoner to these wounds
Until You became my Healer

I was the past versions of myself
That I could not escape
Lost to the noise inside my head
Until You became my way

I was living in chaos
Until Yeshua; You became my Peace
And Abba, my Father, I just want to thank You
For everything You've became for me

Where I've Been

I don't know where I'm going,
But I can tell you where I've been
I've been hurt and abused under the disguise of love
I've been mistreated, rejected, ignored,
All of above

I've been cheated on and abandoned
Hit and called names
I've been told that I'm trash
And should just be thrown away

I've been neglected and cursed at by someone
Who took a vow to stand by my side
I've been talked about behind my back,
Had my vulnerabilities exposed
With no one to turn to as I cried

I've been told to be quiet cause what I thought
Or felt wasn't of any concerned
I've been seen as nothing
But a piece of flesh and not a treasure to be earned

I've been lost and confused,
So, I settled for what was there
I couldn't tell you about the girl looking back
At me in the mirror-her identity wasn't there

I've been in situations that could have killed me,
Cause those people didn't have my back
They just wanted what they could get from me
The men (they) just wanted sex

I've been in places I didn't belong;
Yet they all knew my name
I kept getting my heart hurt,
But had no desire to change

You see; I can't tell you where I'm going
But I can tell you about my Jesus now
About how He met me in my mess
And turned my life around

You see; I can't tell you where I'm going
But I can tell you about the dark places I've been
How I was looking for love in all the wrong places
How I was seeking purity from sin

You see; I can't tell you where I'm going
Cause I've learned to take life day by day
No, I can't tell you where I'm going
But I can tell you
That Daughter of the One True King
Is now my new and forever name.

"Therefore, if any man be in Christ, he is a new creation: old things are passed away, behold, all things become new."

2nd Corinthians 5:17

MY BELOVED

My Beloved
Holds me in His arms
My Beloved
Protects me from harm
My Beloved
Is always near
My Beloved
Wipes away my tears
My Beloved
Has touched my soul
My Beloved
His name: I know
My Beloved
Has healed my heart
My Beloved
From His grace; will never allow me to part
My Beloved
Has walked me through the darkest night
My Beloved
Is surrounding me with His glorious light
My Beloved
Leads me besides still waters
My Beloved
Is my Abba, is my Father
My Beloved
Has washed away my sins
My Beloved
Has allowed a new journey to begin

My Beloved
Covers me and has me apart
My Beloved
Has won me over and is in my heart
My Beloved
Is still writing my story
My Beloved
So I have no need to worry
My Beloved
Walks with me day to day
My Beloved
Has given me a new name
My Beloved
I am His and He is mine
My Beloved
For eternity, for all time.

El-Roi

You are the God who sees me
Even on my worst days
You are the God who sees me
The God who stays

You are the God who sees me
Even when I'm invisible to the world
You are the God who sees me
You've touched my hand and called me Your girl

You are the God who sees me
In the valley, in the wilderness
You are the God who sees me
In my calm, in my mess

You are the God who sees me
Even when I'm surrounded by the dark
You are the God who sees me
Transforming and renewing my heart

You are the God who sees me
From the very beginning, till the end
You are the God who sees me
I am the Daughter of the great I am

You are the God who sees me
You carry me when I'm not strong
You are the God who sees me
Gently teaching me right from wrong

You are the God who sees me
And by the blood of Jesus, I am Your own
You are the God who sees me
I've been adopted into His heavenly home

You are the God who sees me
My Defender, My King
You are the God who sees me
So, to El-Roi; I'll always sing.

My Jesus

My Jesus
Is covered in majesty
My Jesus
Is covered in grace
My Jesus
In a robe of purple and a crown of gold
Oh, behold His glorious face
My Jesus
Mighty and brave
My Jesus
There's no other name
My Jesus
No one is like the Lord of Lords
My Jesus
No one else can save
My Jesus
Holds all power in His hands
My Jesus
Collects all my tears
My Jesus
Chases away the shadows
He calms my fears
My Jesus
Is my beloved
My Jesus
Is my assurance
My Jesus

He is my strength, He is my endurance
My Jesus
Is preparing a place
My Jesus
As He prepares me
My Jesus
The Savior of my life
The One who redeems
My Jesus
Oh; bow down to Him
My Jesus
Give Him praise
My Jesus
Hold on to Him
Always
My Jesus.

You Tell Me

I'm so underserving
Your blood tells me that I'm worthy
I was a lost cause, couldn't find my way
Yet the cross tells me that I'm saved by grace
I was walking around broken, bruised and in despair
Yet, You tell me that Your love
Has always been there
I was living for the flesh and trying
To please the world
Until You came along and told me that I'm Your girl
I had a heart of stone to go along
With living in the flesh
Until You told me, that for my life,
You know what's best
You tell me that I'm forgiven
When the world tells me,
I should be ashamed
You shut the door on my past
And threw the keys away
Lord, You tell me that I'm beautiful
Even when I show You my flaws
You sent my Redeemer Jesus
To catch me when I fall
Now, I'm no longer living by the labels
They once put on me
Cause by Your grace and mercy;
I've been set free

Now I'm walking in the value and identity
Given by the GREAT I AM
It's something so beautiful and so above man
Lord, teach my heart to be still as I sit at Your feet
Cause it's only in Your love that I am complete
Now I'm walking away from what and who
I used to be
And holding on to all the promises You tell me.

She Is

She is
Set apart for His glory
She is
Already a bride
She is
Far above rubies
She is
The one in whom He delights
She is
Followed by grace and mercy
She is
Misunderstood by the world
She is
Called to a different path
She is
Daddy's girl
She is
Seeking His heart daily
She is
The apple of His eye
She is
Called and chosen with a purpose
She is
Seeking His glorious light
She is
Giving up the things of this world

She is
Kneeling before the throne
She is
Making the way through the crowd
She is
Just to touch the hem of His robe
She is
Learning the ways of her Creator
She is
Seeking His face
She is
Holding on to His promises
She is
Giving a new name
She is
Rising above the distractions
She is
Learning to be still
She is
Lead by the Good Shephard
She is
Longing to do His will
She is
Giving herself away to Him
She is
Her imperfections, struggles, and flaws
She is
Learning to be vulnerable with Him

She is

Cause He'll catch her every time she falls

She is

Putting on the full armor

She is

Discovering her worth

She is

Falling in love ever so sweetly

She is

With the One who formed her at birth

She is

A warrior that can move mountains

She is

Anointed by His touch

She is

Evidence of His goodness

She is

Evidence of His love

She is

Trading her wounds for wisdom

She is

Dry bones come alive

She is

Beauty for ashes and grace restored

She is

His bride

She is

Holding on to His promises

She is

No matter what life may bring
She is
Walking in the authority given to her
She is
As the daughter of the One True King!

I Wanna

I wanna see Your face
I wanna hear Your heart
From Your presence Lord
I don't wanna part

So please come hold me close
Take me in Your arms
Cause You are my protector
Defending me from harm

I wanna hear Your voice
So loud, so clear
So quiet these thoughts of mine
And whisper in My ear

Cause You are my strong tower
You are my defense and shield
You go before me and stand behind me
With my life, I just wanna be in Your will

I'll push through the crowd Lord
Just to touch the end of Your robe
Cause within Your hands lie healing
Within Your hands, lies hope

I'll climb the highest tree Father
Just to see You walking by
So please remove the obstacles that come my way
That keeps You from my mind

Let me wash Your feet with my tears, Abba
Let me pour out my all
Cause You have proven time after time
That You'll catch me when I fall

Lead me besides the still waters Lord
Please keep showing me the way
Cause all I wanna do is proclaim Your goodness
Every night; everyday

I wanna hear Your heart Lord
Yes, I wanna see Your face
So please stay by my side
Dear Lord, please stay.

Wonders without Numbers

For my God doesn't slumber
He does wonders without numbers
He chases away the darkness with His light
He brings joy to those who weep at night

For my God never fails
Over death and sin, He has prevailed
In His hands is everlasting life
All that is wrong, He makes right

For my God created the whole Earth
And from the Virgin Mary, was Yeshua birthed
Yes, the Lord of Lords and King of Kings
And salvation, He so beautifully brings

For my God has touched my heart
Has pulled me out of the things
That was keeping us apart
He kept running after me,
Even when I didn't know I was lost
Told me that I was worthy by the sacrifice
On the cross

For my God loves me so
He has healed and consumed my soul
He's wiped away the tears I've cried
Has promised to never leave my side

For my God is so powerful and true
And what He has done for me,
He longs to do for you
My life was headed in the wrong direction
I was living in the flesh till my God stepped in

For my God doesn't slumber
He does wonders without numbers
Call upon His name, let Him into your heart
Don't be deceived, you have been set apart

For my God is amazing and so true
For my God will never abandon you
You won't regret placing your trust in Him
So, say that prayer
And let the spiritual transformation begin.

Based on Job 9:10B

The Fight

I was walking with Jesus
Until the world stepped in
A single rose and a smile
That's where it begins

My heart began to stray
And for my Jesus, my arms no longer reached
Thought I had finally found the one
That was perfection for me

Yet, it was all a lie
All the promises He spoke
So, I set my heart on building my finances
But that chase left me broke

I was consumed by the things of this world
The media and peer pressure
Controlling the way I think
I strayed even more from my Jesus
And in the chaos, I started to drink

But that left me feeling empty
And my friend,
Well, she left me too
The rejection stung me
The rejection just made me more confused

I started comparing myself to others
All I wanted was to fit in
When Ms. Popular came around
I wanted desperately to be her friend

But I didn't look the way she looked
And I didn't dress the way she dressed
My identity had been removed
And I thought she knew what was best

But she walked away too
Just like all the others
By this darkness, I was being consumed
By this pain, I was being smothered

A knife ended up in my hand
Cause I don't know when I last truly smiled
How can I go on
When I haven't called on His name in a while?

A voice whispered "end it all"
And how I almost caved
Until I recalled my Jesus
And the true peace and love He gave

So, I went running back to Him
But so much was standing in the way
But through the fighting, through it all
I could hear Him softly calling my name

But the world kept stepping in
My past wouldn't leave
It kept dragging me down
It didn't want to set me free

But I kept reaching for Jesus
And He was reaching for me too
I had to fight through the pain
Was praying for breakthrough

And that's when I felt His arms around me
As I surrender and fell to my knees
You see, regardless of how far I strayed
My Jesus never stopped fighting for me

He delivered me from the darkness
He delivered me from the pain
He is mine and I am His
And in His presence, I will stay.

Inspired by Lifehouse-Everything (the skit)

I Am (Learning, Transforming, Growing)

And I am learning
To trust God
Even when I am hurting
Cause the pain that I feel doesn't change
Who He is in my life
The circumstances that I go through
Doesn't keep Him from my side
I am learning

And I am learning
To lean on God
When it comes to things that I don't understand
When things don't go the way
That I think they should go
I am learning

And I am learning
That I am still an imperfect mess,
That falls short each day
But by His mercy, by His grace, I am saved
I am learning
To hold on to His beautiful name

And I am growing
From the wounds of the lessons
That I've come to learn
These scars are from being thrown in the fire,
But I did not get burn
I am growing

And I am growing
The closer I get to Him,
The less this world temporarily holds
I can no longer be defined
By anything that didn't create my soul
I am growing

And I am growing
Slowly becoming everything
that He's calling me to be
Transformed by His grace, by His blood, set free
I am growing
And saying farewell to the things I used to serve
Walking in the light and love of His promises
Seeking eternity's door
I am growing

And I am transforming
Cause my Father has given me a new name
So, I no longer wear the labels the world gave me
I am transforming
As He molds and folds me within His hands
Calling me to breathe deeply with a fresh wind
I am transforming

***So, I am EVERYTHING that my Father says of
me and I refuse to go back to the chains that once
held me! I am walking out of Egypt, no longer a
slave! Free in Him cause of the price He paid! I am
learning and holding on to His hands as I go & I am
growing by reading and meditating on His word! I
am transforming. My life is a blank canvas for Him
to do His work! Learning, growing, transforming! A
willing vessel for this end time work!***

Who Am I?

Who am I? In Your eyes Lord
Cause I see the labels the world has put on me
But You tell me that I've been set apart
That You've sealed Your promises in my heart
And that I'm righteously redeemed

Who am I? In Your eyes Lord
Cause I'm so used to being thrown away
But You've shown me a love so unconditional
You've covered me in a love that's here to stay

Who am I? In Your eyes Lord
Cause so many times I'm such a mess
But You've reached down,
Separated me from the crowd
Said, "daughter; we're not done yet"

Who am I? In Your eyes Lord
When I'm afraid to take the next step
You've covered me in grace
Lord, You've broken up these chains
Called me beautiful and gave me a new name

Who am I? In Your eyes Lord
That You would desire to hear from me
You command the wind and waves
Keep the ocean at bay,
And still take the time to speak

Who am I? In Your eyes Lord
That You gave me Your very breathe
I'm redeemed by the blood,
By Your one and only Son
Now it's my desire to hear, "daughter, well done"

Who am I? In Your eyes Lord
That You continue to make a way
Though I stumble and fall,
You're there each time I call
And Lord, I need You
Every night and every day.

Captivated

Captivated
By Your beauty
Captivated
By Your love
Captivated
My Redeemer
You're the only one I'm thinking of
Captivated
By Your mercy
Captivated
By Your goodness
My promise keeper
Daily, I'm walking in Your assurance
Captivated
By Your glory
Captivated
By Your grace
My Savior
As You give me strength from day to day
Captivated
By Your peace
Captivated
By Your mind
Captivated
My healer
You are so kind
Captivated

By Your hands
Captivated
By Your words
My King-You bring beauty to ashes
And healing to hurts
Captivated
By Your forgiveness
Captivated
By Your light
My Father which art in heaven-never leaves me
Even in the darkest of nights
Captivated
By Your heart
Captivated
My Jesus
I'm simply
Captivated
By You.

Awaken Me, Lord

Awaken me Lord
I no longer want to slumber
Speak Lord
Above the storms
A voice like thunder

Awaken me Lord
Call these dry bones to life
Walk with me Lord
Cause I am a conqueror with You by my side

Awaken me Lord
Give me spiritual eyes to see
Guide my steps Lord
For I am Your sheep

Awaken me Lord
And Your name shall be exalted
Hide me Lord
For the enemy comes at me often

Awaken me Lord
For there's much work to do
So, prepare me Lord
For the harvest is ready, but the workers are few

Awaken me Lord
Dress me in Your glory
Touch these lips Lord
And I shall tell of Your story

Awaken me Lord
Dress me in white
I'm so grateful Lord
For my Savior's sacrifice

Awaken me Lord
For You've called me by name
Cover me Lord
In Your mercy, in Your grace

Awaken me Lord
Upon Your promises I will stand
Strengthen me Lord
To do all that I can

Awaken me Lord
For I was created for such a time
Keep me Lord
For I am Yours and You are mine.

Lord

Lord
You found me
Even when I didn't know I was lost
Lord
You saved me
Your son paying the cost
Lord
You've changed me
Touched my heart and gave me a new name
Lord
You've called me
To leave the past behind and I'll never be the same
Lord
You've touched me
From the inside out,
Making a message out of the mess
Lord
You've formed me
From my mother's womb,
So You know me the best
Lord
You're collecting every tear
That slides down my face
Lord
You are restoring all of the years that I have waste
Lord
You are molding

Giving me beauty for ashes
Lord
You are turning
Every trial that I go through into a lesson
Lord
You are my covering
Lord
You are the potter
I am the clay turning into gold
Lord
You are always there
Of this I am sure
Lord
Of heaven-Lord of Earth
Adoni
There is no one like You.

Jesus

Jesus
You loved me
Even when my heart was dark
Jesus
You told me
That from me, You would never part
Jesus
You put me back together as I was falling apart
Jesus
You gave me a fresh, clean start
Jesus
You hold my hand as I walk through the darkness
Jesus
You take the sting out of death
And cloak me in Your softness
Jesus
You are my strength when I can't endure
Jesus
You go before me, of this I'm sure
Jesus
When everyone left, You chose to stay
Jesus
Helping me through these trials as I found the way
Jesus
When You speak, it calms my mind
Jesus
Yes, I am Yours and You are mine

Jesus
Even when the answer seems unclear
Jesus
I keep moving forward, cause You are near
Jesus
You've called these dry bones to rejoice again
Jesus
As You paid the price that washed away my sin
Jesus
It's in Your presence that I long to stay
Jesus
You truly are the light, the truth, and the way
Jesus
Please keep walking with me.
I don't want to do this alone
Jesus
Please come into my heart and highlight this soul
Jesus
Everything that I am can be found in You
Jesus
My identity, my value; yes-it's true
Jesus
Thank You for calling these dry bones alive
Jesus
Thank You for being the fourth man
In the fire every time

Jesus
You are the Good Shephard, and I will follow Your
lead
Jesus
Thank You for loving me.

The One

What could I ever give?
For the One whom gave His life for me?
The One who went to the cross
To beautifully set me free

What could I ever offer?
To the One whom gave it all
The One who's been by my side
Faithfully, through it all

What could I ever say?
About the One who transformed my heart
Who meet me when I was at my lowest
And held me as I was falling apart

What could I ever do?
For the One in whose image I am made
Who has walked me through the darkness
And covered me in His grace

What could I ever sing?
About the One whom delights in me
The One who touched these chains
And out of bondage, set me free

What could I ever proclaim?
Let all that I am point the way back to the One
That loved me when I didn't even love myself
That proclaimed that the battle's already been won

What could I ever sacrifice?
To the One whose blood has made me new
So Yeshua, I pray that my life
Points the way back to You.

Make a Sweet, Sweet Sound

All of heaven make a sweet, sweet sound
Bend the knee, cast the crown

For the King of Glory is on His throne
What beauty and sight to behold!

All of Earth shout and sing
For deliverance the Savior brings

Blow the trumpet and pluck the harp
For He has come to set us apart

Lift up Your voices and cast your cares
Look to the hills, for He is there!

For all of creation groans and waits
For the clouds to part on that day

For demons flee at the power in that name
One encounter with Him
And you'll never be the same

Oh, praise Him my heart! Oh, praise Him my soul!
Shout it from the mountains,
I'll let my testimony be known!

Oh, how He saved me from a life of darkness
Oh, how He softened me and took away this
hardness

I was a stiff neck sinner gratifying the flesh
Always seeking more while settling for less

I was married to the world
While satan was in my ear
He whispered, "a little bit of witchcraft
Won't hurt anyone, my dear"

Oh, how I believed the lies from the father of all lies
Oblivious that he was after this soul of mine

But even in my unbelief, my Jesus was there
There is a cross and an empty grave
To prove that He cares

So now I bend my knees and cast my crown
Rejoice with creation
And make a sweet, sweet sound

Cause my Savior has made me whole
Cause my Savior is a beautiful sight to behold

So, I will shout and I will sing
Of all the goodness and mercy He brings

I'll blow the trumpet and pluck the harp
I'll give my all to the One who has set me apart

Yes, this is my story, this is my song
And I'll worship my Savior all the day long.

Our Father Which Art in Heaven

Our Father which art in heaven
Thank You for this day
Our Father which art in heaven
Thank You for making a way

Our Father which art in heaven
Thank You for Your peace
Our Father which art in heaven
Thank You for saving me

Our Father which art in heaven
With endless mercy and endless grace
Our Father which art in heaven
Thank You for giving me a new name

Our Father which art in heaven
All power belongs to You
Our Father which art in heaven
You are the way, the light, the truth

Our Father which art in heaven
Thank You for wiping away these tears
Our Father which art in heaven
You're never far, but always near

Our Father which art in heaven
Thank You for causing these lungs to breathe
Our Father which art in heaven
You saw my brokenness and healed me

Our Father which art in heaven
Thank You for pulling me out of the dark
Our Father which art in heaven
Thank You for softening this heart

Our Father which art in heaven
Who knows the beginning as well as the end
Our Father which art in heaven
Thank You for coming to my rescue time and time
again

Our Father which art in heaven
How beautiful is Your name?
Our Father which art in heaven
You lead me besides still waters and there I'll stay

Our Father which art in heaven
Thank You for being by My side
Our Father which art in heaven
I am Yours and You are mine.

The Woman with the Issue of Blood

Unclean is what they call me
Unclean has become my new name
Ever since I've had this issue
Ever since, it won't go away

Undeserving is what they call me
She's bearing the weight of her sin
I hear them whisper as they walk by
As I'm overlooked once again

Unworthy is what they tell me
This issue, leading me to be cast out
A reject, a nobody
That no one has tried to figure out

I can't recall the last time I've smiled
My joy and peace have been stolen
I can't recall what normal used to be
Nor how it feels to be golden

I've been left along with this issue
No cure could be found
Spent all I had seeking answers
Spent it all, with nothing to count

My livelihood is nonexistent
I am a prisoner in my own home
There's no way to escape my flesh
I am bound and sadden in my soul

Until one day I saw the crowd gather
There was a shift in the air
I looked distantly at what was happening
And rumor was Yeshua was there

The people had already ostracized me
So, I started to crawl to make my way through
It's easy to remain hidden when they choose not to
see
But I had an urge of what I needed to do

Cause you see, I had tried everything that I knew
But found the courage to try once more
To fall upon my knees and find a way
To the One that they adore

The dirt and rocks dug into my skin
But I wanted to be set free
Of this issue that kept me bound
So, for His hem, I did reach

Just a touch and warmth entered my body
Just a touch and the issue was gone
I tremble, I cried at the release
For 12 years, this issue had gone on

I heard the Master ask "who touched Me"
And quietly and with fear, I replied
Couldn't lift up my head to meet His majesty
No, couldn't look Him in the eye

There was silence all around us
It was truly a sight to behold
He smiled beautifully and stated
"Daughter, your faith has made you whole"

On this day my joy has been restored
On this day I have been healed
The woman with the issue of blood
Is just part of my story
Cause now I have a testimony that is so real

I implore you my sweet friend
To find your way to Yeshua too
Whatever issue, whatever is keeping you bound
He has healing just for you.

*** Mark 5:25-34 ***

The Reality of it All

The reality of it all
Is that life sometimes catches us by surprise
The reality of it all
Is that we live, that we die

The reality of it all
We'll have moments of laughter, moments of pain
The reality of it all
Is that we don't know what tomorrow may bring

The reality of it all
Is that life isn't always simple
And sometimes the answers aren't clear
The reality of it all
Is that the people that we were once close to
Aren't always near

The reality of it all
We'll have seasons in the valley,
Seasons on the mountain tops
The reality of it all
Is that God never changes,
And regardless of what we go through,
His promises will never stop

The reality of it all
Is that we all need someone
That will take us by the hand
The reality of it all
To navigate through the trials of this life,
Someone who truly understands

The reality of it all
Is that sometimes life breaks us,
And sometimes kicks us while we're down
The reality of it all
Is that there in our brokenness, God's grace is found

The reality of it all
Is that life keeps moving forward,
Despite how we feel
The reality of it all
Is that sometimes we have to say to our souls,
"Peace-be still"

The reality of it all
Is that we all have a beginning,
We all have an end
The reality of it all
But God writes our stories-yes, He holds the pen

The reality of it all
Is that no matter what we go through, God is there
The reality of it all
Is that our Abba Father, He truly cares

The reality of it all
Is that His love pieces back together
The things that broke
The reality of it all
Is that within Him, there is peace.
With Jesus, there is hope

The reality of it all
Is that He is returning for His bride one day
The reality of it all
And every tear, He shall beautifully wipe away.

Dedicated to: My sister. May you rest in peace.

He Left the 99

He left the 99
To be by my side
Yes, His love ran after me
And now I am set free

He left the 99
And called my name
He left the 99
Sin and darkness
Couldn't stand in the way

He left the 99
And traveled through the dark
He corrected my wrongs
And mended my heart

He left the 99
And carried me to His throne
Called me His daughter
And gave me a new home

He left the 99
And saved me as I was lost
The veil was torn in two
So heavy, the cost

He left the 99
And leads me besides still waters
He guides me beautifully
He won't let me falter

He left the 99
And set my feet on solid ground
And in His mercy, in His grace
His love abounds

He left the 99
And wiped away my shame
Gave me beauty for ashes
I'll never be the same

He left the 99
And rescued me
Paid the ultimate price
To set me free.

His

His brokenness
Made me whole
His faithfulness
Saved my soul
His voice
Calls my name
His love
Left me changed
His hands
Have touched my heart
From His affection
I'm never apart
His life
Spared my own
His sacrifice
Washed me whole
His cross
Was mine to bear
He took my burdens
He took my cares
Of His grace
I'm so underserving
To look upon His face
I am yearning
His stripes
In exchange for my sins
Crucified

So, I may live
His promises
Always true
His strength
Always carries me through
He was hurt
So, I could be healed
And of Holy Spirit
I am sealed
He is
Assurance
When I have doubts
From beginning to end
He has it all figured out
He is truth
In a world that is fake
He is the light
He is the way
He is
My Comforter
That brings me peace
Of my shames, He has set me free
He is mine
And I am His
Simply
Beautifully
His.

Hey Sis

Hey sis
God hasn't forgotten about you
Hey sis
God hears your prayers
Hey sis
You are fearfully and wonderfully made
Hey sis
You are the head and not the tail
Hey sis
You are righteously redeemed
Hey sis
God's favor is upon your life
Hey sis
I'm sorry they hurt you, but God wants to heal you
Hey sis
You don't have to carry the weight of the world
Hey sis
You don't have to live up to other people's
expectations
Hey sis
Let them talk about who you used to be, the right
ones see who God is calling you to be
Hey sis
Don't let the enemies lies overshadow God's truth
Hey sis
YOU'RE BEAUTIFUL JUST AS YOU ARE

Hey sis
You are the apple of His eye
Hey sis
You are close to His heart
Hey sis
God is still writing your story, so stop letting other
people narrate it
Hey sis
God will make that broken beautiful
Hey sis
He'll give you beauty for ashes
Hey sis
Joy comes in the morning
Hey sis
The best is yet to come
Hey sis
God's got you
Hey sis
You were never forsaken, you've always been held
by God
Hey sis
HE LOVES YOU
WITH AN EVERLASTING LOVE.

(This is) To the Girl

This is to the girl
Who's surrounded by people but feels so alone
This is to the girl
Who feels like a stranger in her own home

This is to the girl
Who in a world that's so loud,
Struggles to find her own voice
This is to the girl
Who's been knocked down and mistreated
Not by choice

This is to the girl
That won't look in the mirror
Cause she's afraid of what she'll see
This is to the girl
Who's going along with the trend
Cause she lost her own identity

This is to the girl
Who's been melting on the inside
While playing it cool
This is to the girl
Who more than once, has been fooled

This is to the girl
Who's lost track of how many tears she's cried
This is to the girl
Who hides so much on the inside

This is to the girl
That can't escape those awful memories
This is to the girl
Who keeps thinking about what used to be

This is to the girl
Who's been told she's not good enough
This is to the girl
That when she cried, she was told to toughen up

This is to the girl
Who's there for others while she falls apart
This is to the girl
That has a beautiful yet shattered heart

This is to the girl
That fades into the shadow and is misunderstood
This is to the girl
Who was bullied throughout all of school

This is to the girl
That chooses to rise up despite it all
This is to the girl
That gets pushed to the side but refuses to fall

This is to the girl
That wakes up every day and keeps marching ahead
This is to the girl
That walks into the new
While walking away from what's dead

This is to the girl
Who so beautifully wears her scars
Cause she knows one day
They will be traded for a crown
This is to the girl
That silences out the noise of the world
And focuses on making her Father proud

This is to the girl
That isn't afraid to tell her story
Of how, because of Jesus
She now worships instead of worry

This is to the girl
Who holds her head high because she knows
That she is not of this world
And that His DNA is in her soul.

This is to the girl.

Made New

He clothed me in garments of His glory
And removed my garments of shame
He told me that I had a different story
And that my life wouldn't end this way

He chipped away at this heart of stone
He gave me this heart of flesh
He kissed the wounds that life gave me
And told me that He knows what's best

He grabbed my hand as I was living in the dark
He pulled me out of the mess I made
He took the shattered pieces of my heart
And tenderly wiped every single tear away

He told me that He never stopped loving me
Even when I had stopped loving Him
He told me that I am His sheep
And that He'll run after me time and time again

It's His love that keeps me in perfect peace
It's His promises that sees me through
He's strong enough to calm the storms at sea
And ever so faithful to see me through

And on the mountain tops or in the valleys
My Savior has made my path clear
He has promised that neither life nor death
Will keep Him from being near

The One who created the whole world
Also created me, so I must be beautiful in His sight
He exhaled and now I can breathe
And He tells me that I am His delight

He holds my hand and I won't let go
He's locked eyes with me,
And I don't want to look away
I'm no longer wearing the weight
Of who I used to be
My Abba Father has given me a new name

Now, I long to be an extension of Him
Until He calls me home
Now, I know why I am here
To introduce others to His throne.

God's Masterpiece

I am God's masterpiece
Created by His hand
Formed into creation
By the rib of man

I am God's masterpiece
Yes, He had me on His mind
Before the world was created
Before the beginning of time

I am God's masterpiece
He loves me with all of His heart
From His love, from His affection
I shall never part

I am God's masterpiece
Fearfully and wonderfully made
He is the potter
I am the clay

I am God's masterpiece
He calls me His daughter
I hold tightly to His hand
Cause He is a good, good Father

I am God's masterpiece
His ways, I long to know
To forsake the things of this world
And to love Him with all of my soul

I am God's masterpiece
And He hears when I call His name
He saved me when I was at my lowest
And I'll never ever be the same

I am God's masterpiece
And now, I can finally see
How He is writing my story
And only has good plans for me

I am God's masterpiece
From His truth, I'll never stray
Sent His Son to rewrite my story
Sent His Son, Yeshua is His name

I am God's masterpiece
Wasn't created to fit into this world
Created to tell my story
Of how and why I'm a Daddy's girl

I am God's masterpiece
And He has wiped away every tear
He brings me peace in the storm
He brings calm to my fears

I am God's masterpiece
Of this, I have assurance
And Yahweh, I just want to thank You
For Your mercy and goodness.

***Hey sis,

The Creator of the whole earth looked down before the beginning of time and decided that He wanted you here. 🖤 No, it didn't happen by chance, nor by luck, and definitely not by mistake (so stop letting the enemy tell you that you are one). He had you on His mind and dreamed of in His heart before your parents, grandparents, etc. even took their first breath. He knitted and formed you in your mother's womb and had a plan for you from the start. If you have been feeling lost lately, find your way to Him. If you've been believing the lies for a while now, find the truth in Him. If you've been a girlfriend to the darkness/sin that so freely runs this world, then it's time to run back to your first love and get married to the light and allow Him to wash and make you whole. If you've been identifying yourself by the world's standards, get in the word. Read and learn about who God says you are (this world is against everything of Him and tries to make it look good). Remember, you were never created to live alone. You have a Father in heaven that has called you by name and adores you. He tells me that you are far above rubies. He tells me that you are the one in whom He delights in. He tells me that you are the apple of His eye. You are so beautifully loved by Him, so stay right there. Allow Him to hold your hand and guide your steps. He will never mislead you. For you are, we are His. I am the daughter of the great I Am and sis, so are you.

You Are Loved

You are loved with a love
That pierces the darkest of dark
You are loved with a love
That mends the most broken of hearts
You are loved with a love
That washes and makes new
You are loved with a love
Fully consumed
You are loved with a love
That most can't understand
You are loved with a love
Stronger and greater than any man
You are loved with a love
That will carry you through the pain
You are loved with a love
That has the power to take the guilt away
You are loved with a love
That is freely given and overflows
You are loved with a love
That intermingles with your soul
You are loved with a love
That nothing can separate
You are loved with a love
That calls you by name
You are loved with a love
That will guide your every step
You are loved with a love
That took away the sting of death

74

You are loved with a love
That is holding you so tight
You are loved with a love
That will make everything that's wrong, right
You are loved with a love
That will not be moved
You are loved with a love
That knows the core of you
You are loved with a love
That's full of hope, full of peace
You are loved with a love
For all of eternity.

Father God,

I thank You for Your love. I thank You that You
teach us how to love. I thank You that Your love is
freely given and not affected by time, distance,
circumstance, or my emotions. Father God, I thank
You that in a world that is constantly shaking, that
You are unshakable. Thank You for being my rock,
thank You for being my sword, thank You for being
my strength. I open my heart to receive Your love
and as I receive Your love Father, I pray that it
overflows into others.

In Yeshua's name,
Amen

Love Came Down

Love came down and wrapped me in His arms
Said, daughter you are Mine and I'll protect you
from harm

Love came down to heal and to make me whole
To show me my value and to touch my soul

Love came down and covered my shames
Chased away the darkness and gave me a new name

Love came down and looked me in the eyes
Said I am your promise keeper that will never leave
your side

Love came down and now I can truly see
Just how this world had a hold on me

Love came down full of mercy and grace
I had to learn to be still to hear Him calling my
name

Love came down and is leading me beside still
waters
Gave me His peace cause I am His daughter

Love came down to guide me to the straight and
narrow path
All things are fleeting, but with Him-it shall last

Love came down to write a different story
And now I worship instead of worry

Love came down to teach my soul to be still
And now I long to be in my Father's will

Love came down to truly set me apart
That's how I know that He has touched my heart.

Psalm 43

Judge me, O God
For only Your judgments are right
When I oppose what's popular
The people want to fight

And plead my cause against an ungodly nation
Lord, give them eyes to see
That just because the world says it's okay
That they don't have to agree

O deliver me from the deceitful and unjust man
Who thinks I have hate in my heart
Simply speaking Your truth Lord
Has torn so many apart

For thou are the God of my strength
Without You, I am weak
Please allow me to abide in You
Please continue to abide in me

Why dost thou cast me off?
Lord, I truly try
Even when temptation is in my face
To do that which is right

Why go I mourning?
When joy is on the way
So, I will focus on Your promises
And the hope that they bring

Because of the oppression of the enemy
Fear and anxiety have tried to creep in
But fear is not my portion
So, I shall rejoice once again

O send out thy light and thy truth
So, others will understand
That wisdom comes from you
Knowledge for man

Let them lead me
O Lord, let them lead
Just want to follow the path
That You have laid out for me

Let them bring me unto thy holy hill
May I rejoice in who You are
You have saved me from my sins
And You are always near, never far

And to thy tabernacles Lord
In that still small place
Where I can turn off the noise of the world
And humbly seek thou face

Then I will go into the altar of God
With joy and gladness in my heart
For once Jesus has chosen you
From you, He shall never part

Unto God my exceeding joy
Who has the perfect plan for me
Who is the author of my soul
And still writing my story

Yea, upon the harp I will praise thee
I will give You all of my praise
You are the God of miracles
You are the God that makes a way

O God, my God
Who has fashioned and knitted me in my mother's womb
Lord, I am nothing. Lord, I am no one
No, not without You

Why art thou cast down?
I'll look up and praise Your name
My God is still winning battles
My God is still mighty to save

O, my soul
Let us dance and sing
O, my soul
To the king of kings

And why art thou disquieted within me?
We must not give the rocks a reason to shout
We must make boldly known the gospel
And just what Jesus is about

Hope in God
And truly try to get to know
The One who created you
The only One who can make you whole

For I shall yet praise Him
For I am made new
Crucified with the old
And seeing all things new

Who is the health of my countenance?
Yes, my God keeps me strong
Even when I feel weak
Through Him, I keep on

And my God
Who has His eyes upon me
And my God
Perfect and true
God, I thank You
Just for being You.

(Help My) Unbelief

Help my unbelief Lord
For the enemy is in my ear
Help my unbelief Lord
I want to keep Your truth near

Help my unbelief Lord
Cause my insecurities are on the rise again
Help my unbelief Lord
Before the doubt settles in

Help my unbelief Lord
To hold on, I'm trying my best
Help my unbelief Lord
Cause my faith is being put to the test

Help my unbelief Lord
Cause Your promises seem so far away
Help my unbelief Lord
Cause I'm feeling a bit fragile today

Help my unbelief Lord
This situation is much too deep
Help my unbelief Lord
Cause this heaviness, I don't want to keep

Help my unbelief Lord
This isn't the way my life as supposed to go
Help my unbelief Lord
I was tossed aside and bought low

Help my unbelief Lord
Cause this wound just keeps getting bigger
Help my unbelief Lord
And those that judge me, keep pointing their finger

Help my unbelief Lord
Cause my mind won't let go of these thoughts
Help my unbelief Lord
I want to surrender, whatever the cost

Help my unbelief Lord
There are so many pieces of my life
That's been shattered
Help my unbelief Lord
And with Your hands, please put me back together

Help my unbelief Lord
I've traveled a long way to arrive
At the end of Your robe
Help my unbelief Lord
Speak Abba, to these dry bones

Help my unbelief Lord
And be the glory within my mist
Help my unbelief Lord
Cause I was born for such a time as this.

*"And straightway the Father of the child cried out,
and he said with tears, Lord, I believe, help thou
mine unbelief."*
Mark 9:24

*"And who knoweth whether thou art come to the
kingdom for such a time as this"*
Esther 4:14B

*"When she heard of Jesus, came in the press behind
and touched His garment. For she said, if I may
touch but His clothes, I shall be whole."*
Mark 5:27-28

*"The hand of the Lord was upon me, and carried
me out into the Spirit of the Lord, and sat me down
in the midst of the valley which was full of bones,
and caused me to pass by them round about; and
behold, there were very many in the open valley;
and lo, they were very dry."*
Ezekiel 37:1-2

Finally

I took the long way around, but I'm finally here
After much heartache and crying many tears

There were so many lessons that I had to learn
So much that I tolerated that I didn't deserve

There's been seasons where I've had to crawl but
I'm finally standing
Took off the garment of mourning and now I am
laughing

So many past layers have melted away
The old version of me is in the grave

I used to not know who I was, but now,
I can finally say
That I'm a Daddy's girl
And fearfully and wonderfully made

I poured out at His feet my alabaster jar
Showed Him my broken, my ugly, my scars

He handed me a rose and said that I'm finally free
Whispered in my ear
That He never stopped chasing after me

He said He was there in the silence,
And there in the pain
Was reaching out for me, even when I looked away

And I'm stepping into His promises
Cause I'm finally no longer broken
The darkness has to flee
Cause my Abba Father has spoken

I've been made new by the price Jesus paid
I've forsaken the world,
It's in His love that I want to stay

You see, I used to chase the things of this world,
But finally, I've learned to be still
And now it is my desire to be in my Father's will

I was the reason that the ninety-nine,
He had to leave
So, Abba Father, I thank You for the finally.

Prayer:

Father God,
I thank You Lord. I thank You for sending Your only begotten Son while I was yet still a sinner. I thank You for growing me, transforming me, and challenging me. I thank You for the finally. For Your long-suffering Lord, through all my mistakes, failures, and wrong turns that I took. Thank You for always showing up for me. I love You.

In Jesus name,
Amen

Why Don't You

Why don't you lay that burden down?
You've been carrying it for awhile
I've been walking beside you with my hands
outstretched
I've been walking beside you-bidding you to rest

I've felt your heartache
And I've seen your tears
Just one prayer
And you would know that I'm here

I've been watching you fight battles
That wasn't yours to fight
I hear the racing thoughts
That keep you up at night

Why don't you lift up your head, Child
And seek My face
For I am never the one
That walks away

I long to walk with you
But do you long to walk with Me?
Within My name
You can be set free

I'm with you when you're happy
I'm with you when you're sad
Don't you remember
The connection we once had?

Why don't you trust Me with your today?
Trust Me with all of your tomorrows
For I am the way
I am the healing for your sorrow

Just slow down my beautiful one
Slow down and see
My hands outstretched
Towards thee

Behold, I stand at the door and knock
Won't you let Me in?
It's time to pick up your cross
And let the faith journey begin.

"Casting all your care upon him, for He careth for you."
1ST Peter 5:7

"Then said Jesus unto His disciples, if any man will come after Me, let him deny himself, and take up his cross, and follow me."
Matthew 16:24

The Lord Shall

The Lord shall teach my soul to be still
As the storms in my life rage
The Lord shall hold my hand through these battles,
making me brave

The Lord shall speak peace to my soul
As He leads me besides still waters
The Lord shall hide me behind the shadow
Of His right hand cause I am His daughter

The Lord shall fight for me
When I'm fragile and afraid
The Lord shall rebuke the spirit of fear
And in His light, I shall stay

The Lord shall order my steps
When the path seems unclear
I will walk by faith cause I know He is near

The Lord shall restore what the locusts ate
And redeem the time
As He whispers softly in my ear, "Daughter, you are
Mine!"

The Lord shall create in me a clean heart
And renew within me a righteous spirit
To clearly hear His voice,
You've got to let go of religion

The Lord shall hear my voice
When I call His name
Cause of the relationship
We have that the blood of Jesus gave

The Lord shall never turn His back on me,
Cause His promises are true
I desire to be clean and He has made me new

The Lord shall remind me of who I am
On the days that I cannot recall
His hand is upon my life,
Ready to catch me when I fall

The Lord shall cover me with His banner,
Cover me with His grace
The anointing comes from heaven
And nothing can take its place

The Lord shall allow me to find Him
As I seek Him with my whole heart
His arms hold me together
When it all seems to fall apart

The Lord shall give me a reason to smile
In the midst of crying
I am a Daddy's girl
And to please Him so, I am trying

The Lord shall allow me to forget the former things
As He redeems my story
Now I praise Him from a place of victory
And declare, Abba, You get the glory

The Lord shall be the sustainer of all my needs,
He won't allow His daughter to settle for less
Cause it is true what they say,
Daddy always knows best.

Nothing but the Blood of Jesus

Nothing but the blood of Jesus
That has washed and made me new
Nothing but the blood of Jesus
That's given me a clear view

Nothing but the blood of Jesus
That has transformed and changed my heart
Nothing but the blood of Jesus
That tore the veil in two,
So that we would never be apart

Nothing but the blood of Jesus
That gives me grace from day to day
Nothing but the blood of Jesus
Even demons tremble at His name

Nothing but the blood of Jesus
That pulled me out of the dark
Nothing but the blood of Jesus
That has given me a new heart

Nothing but the blood of Jesus
That chases the darkness away
Nothing but the blood of Jesus
That is the truth, the light, and the way

Nothing but the blood of Jesus
That helps keep me on the straight and narrow path
Nothing but the blood of Jesus
That will always last

Nothing but the blood of Jesus
The price for my sin
Nothing but the blood of Jesus
On the third day, He rose again

Nothing but the blood of Jesus
That keeps me standing, keeps me strong
Nothing but the blood of Jesus
That helps me to see right from wrong

Nothing but the blood of Jesus
Has the power to transform
Nothing but the blood of Jesus
That can withstand any storm

Nothing but the blood of Jesus
That heals and makes me whole
Nothing but the blood of Jesus
That speaks to my dry bones

Nothing but the blood of Jesus
That allows me to kneel before the throne
Nothing but the blood of Jesus
He calls me His own

Nothing but the blood of Jesus
The Savior of this world
Nothing but the blood of Jesus
Now I can boldly say, yes, I am a Daddy's girl.

The Lord can be Found

The Lord can be found in the hallelujah
As you fully give Him praise
The Lord can be found in the valley
In the deepest parts of your pain

The Lord can be found in the yes and amen
All of His promises are true
The Lord can be found in the brokenness
In the scattered pieces inside of you

The Lord can be found in the chaos
As you lay it all down at His feet
The Lord can be found in the surrender
Within the echo of your heartbeat

The Lord can be found in the laughter
For He is always there
The Lord can be found in the whisper
In your soft, tender prayer

The Lord can be found in the loneliness
In the moments that no one sees
The Lord can be found within
He desires to set you free

The Lord can be found in the beauty
Of the normal of day to day

The Lord can be found in the details
As you surrender to His ways

The Lord can be found in the yesterdays
When you didn't know how you'd make it through
The Lord can be found in your weakness
That's when His strength carries you

The Lord can be found closely
For He doesn't walk away
The Lord can be found within arm's reach
By your side, He longs to stay.

In His Arms

In His arms is where I desire to be
I'm shielded from the world
When I'm with my Daddy

He is my safe place, my shelter, and I'm secured
I am protected heavenly, of this I am sure

When I'm in His arms,
The enemy cannot reach
Abba knocks him down and declares,
"She is Mine to keep"

I am covered in the warmth of His presence
As He hold me close
When I feel that I'm less,
He reassures me the most

He gently hums in my ear
As I lean back and lean in
I was on His mind before time even began

Abba is my love story.
A love that the world cannot create
The movies have tried,
But it's all pretend, it's all fake

Abba holds my hands,
He walks me besides still waters
He speaks to my soul and tells me I'm His daughter

So many have left me,
But my Daddy has stayed by my side
He speaks to who I am, the apple of His eye

Within His arms, there is comfort, there is peace
I drink from the cup that He has filled for me

I run into His arms, with my wounds, with my pains
And just like a good parent, He kisses the hurt away

Yes, He leads and guides me and always protects
He saw me at my worst
And still thought I was the best

So, I'll run into His arms every chance that I get
Cause there's no better feeling
Than knowing that I'm His

He's my all and all, He's my saving grace
And Daddy, in Your arms;
Your daughter longs to stay.

Encouragements

Forgive Them Sis

Forgive
So, you can have peace again
Forgive
So, you can have a sound mind again
Forgive
So, you're no longer a prisoner to that moment,
To the pain they caused, nor to the lies they told
Forgive them sis
So that bitterness won't have a place to take root
Forgive them sis
Don't let what happened define you
Don't let what happened destroy you
Don't let what happened distract you
Forgive them sis
The closer you draw to Christ,
The more those enemy will use people
To come against you
Remember, it's all spiritual and not personal
Forgive them sis
Place it in God's hand and walk away
Forgive them sis
And focus on what and who is ahead of you
And not what and who got left behind
Forgive them sis
Forgive
Release that stronghold
And find happiness once again

Forgive
And let God use you to be an example
Of what grace looks like
Forgive
God will fight your battles,
Just keep your eyes on Him
Forgive
Forgive them sis.

Jesus isn't Afraid of Your Mess

I just wanted to remind you that Jesus
Isn't afraid of your mess
He's not going to run and hide from your tears.
He sees the things that you're going through
And He cares about you.
He knows the truth about that situation,
About that person and how they treated you.
Don't mask the hurt
He wants to heal you
If you're feeling like a failure, you're not
If you're feeling like you're worthless,
Nope-not the truth
Even when we make things worse for ourselves,
Harder for ourselves-as well as others-
When we give it to Jesus,
He does with it what we can't
He untangles the things we've gotten tangled in
He cleans up the messes we find ourselves in
He comes in and lifts up and takes away
The heaviness of the things that we carry
But He can't take it away
Unless we are willing to give it to Him
And that takes being honest
And that takes being real
And that takes being transparent and humble
So be all of those things with Him

He will never use your failures, weaknesses,
Insecurities against you
Jesus found me in my mess,
And I've never been the same
I was walking with darkness
Until the light (Jesus) stepped in
So, let Him do what only He can do
Jesus isn't afraid of your mess.

A Heavenly Reminder (part 1)
You are Loved

I was talking to God this morning and asked Him, "Lord, what would you like for me to share with Your daughters/ my sisters God?"

And His response, "Tell them that I love them and that I want to love on them, and that My love will help them get through this."

So, sis,

This is your reminder that YOU ARE LOVED so fiercely, so strongly, and so consuming by our God. From the moment that you rise till you lay your head down at night, His love is covering you. It is His love that paves a way for you and holds you together when it feels as though your world is falling apart. Can't you feel His arms around you right now? It's that warmth that fills your heart, it's that small whisper that speaks to you, and it's that beautiful butterfly that passed by you....and yet, His love for you is so much more than all of those things.

Romans 8:38 states that nothing can separate us from the Love of our Father. His love is always standing, never shaken, and all consuming...like a fire that can never be put out. How great and how deep the love the Father has for you sis! And I pray that the more that you walk with Him, the more that you talk with Him, and the more that you lean on and trust Him, (regardless of what the situation may look like), that the more you'll feel His love. His love for you has no ending sis, so just stay right there sis.

Stay right there in the middle of the depth of His love for you. Allow that love to chase away every negative thought, every doubt, every lie and opinion spoken over you. Let His love hold and guide you. After all, YOU ARE daddy's little girl. So, receive the love He has for you sis. Receive it fully, receive it expectantly, and receive it gracefully.

YOU ARE loved by our King, and it is such a beautiful thing.
HE LOVES YOU WITH AN UNFAILING LOVE.

A Heavenly Reminder (part 2)
You are Precious in His Sight

I was talking to God this morning and asked Him, "Lord, what would you like for me to share with Your daughters/my sisters God?"

His responded with a still small whisper, "Tell My daughters that they are precious in My sight, a beauty to behold, and that they are secured in My hands."

So, my most amazing and beautiful sisters, be still and hear what thus says the Lord:

Before the foundations of the Earth, I have loved you and called you by name. YOU ARE MINE and I AM YOURS. You are held so securely, so carefully, and so intentionally and delicately in My hands…. that no matter what life may throw your way, as long as you stay within my embrace, the storms of life won't shake you.

Remember, to keep Your eyes on me, not the storm. My precious daughter, I created you fearlessly and wonderfully in My image. Where you see shortcomings, I see grace. Where you see failures, I see an opportunity for your faith and trust in Me to step in and grow.

When the enemy is messing with your mind or playing with your heart and emotions, please open up My word and see what I have to say about you in *Song of Solomon*. My daughter, I say, *"You are altogether beautiful, My love, there is no flaw in you."* (*chapter 4:7*) My daughter, I say that, *"I am my beloved's and my beloved is mine."* (*chapter 6:3*) My daughter, let your response to me be *Song of Solomon 3:4, "I have found the one whom my soul loves."*

So, let my love carry you daughter. My love will carry you through the good days, the bad days, the good moments, the bad moments, the unsure, and sad moments. Call upon your Abba Father, for I always there. Remember, my highly favored and chosen one that you are precious and honored in my sight and I love you (*Isaiah 43:4a.*) Don't let this world keep you busy enough, stress enough, disconnected enough that you don't hear My voice calling your name. For the GREAT I AM IS ALWAYS WITH YOU.

Signed,

The One has called you by name

A Heavenly Reminder (part 3)
I'm Still Here

I was talking to God this morning and asked Him,
"Lord, what would you like for me to share with
Your daughters/my sisters God?"
And in that still small voice, He replied, "Tell My
daughters that I'm still here."

Daughter,

I know that you are hurting, but I'm still here
I know that things aren't going the way you'd like
for them to go, but I'm still here
I know you've been feeling overwhelmed,
overlooked, and underappreciated, but I'm still here
Your heart has been heavy
Mind full of worry
It's been hard to find rest
But I'm still here
In the midst of the rejection, I'm still here
Through all these changes, and the challenges that
life has thrown at you lately, I'm still here
Even in your silence, when you have no words to
express how you feel, My daughter-I'm still here
and I hear you.... even when you don't speak.
Your tears have their own language and speak to Me
Your exhaustion taps me on My shoulder and
speaks to Me

When your heart is breaking, I catch the pieces in My hands, and they speak to Me
You are Mine and even when in your silence, you speak to Me
Remember My child, that there is always a breaking before a breakthrough, there is always a test before a testimony, and sometimes I have to break your heart in order to save your soul. Trust that Father knows what is best for you.
I'm still here. My child and I will calm the storms in your life and bring calm in the midst of the chaos. Just take My hand and call out to me. I love you and I adore you. You are mine and, ALWAYS, I'M STILL HERE. I'm just a prayer away.

Signed,

"The One who will never leave nor forsake you"
Hebrews 13:5
Your Abba Father

"Come unto Me, all ye that labor and are heavy laden, and I will give you rest."
Matthew 11:28

A Heavenly Reminder (part 4)
I AM the GREAT I AM

I was talking to God this morning and asked Him,
"Lord, what would you like for me to share with
Your daughters/ my sisters God?"
And in that still small voice, He replied, "Tell My
daughters that I AM the GREAT I AM."

Pause for a moment sis, clear your mind and make
room for what thus says our heavenly Abba Father:

I AM the GREAT I AM
And since I AM the GREAT I AM, you can face any
and all challenges that may come your way
I AM the GREAT I AM
I go before you, stand behind you, and send My
angels to watch over you
I AM the GREAT I AM
And since I AM the GREAT I AM, you are set to be
everything that I have created you to be. My
daughter, you were birth with a purpose and destiny
lies within your bones
I AM the GREAT I AM
I AM still parting the red sea
I AM still slaying Goliath
I AM still making water come forth from a rock
Just keep your eyes on Me, My Child

And you will behold the marvelous wonders that I
have done and will continue to do
I AM leading you beside still waters
I AM still calling your name
I AM Alpha and Omega, beginning and the end
I AM still writing your story. So, let others have
their opinions about you, I speak truth and promises
over you
I AM the GREAT I AM
I AM your Healer
I AM your Redeemer
I AM your Shield and Strong tower
I AM your Peace and Joy
I AM wiping away your tears
I AM turning your heartache into healing, rejection
into redirection, and tears into laughter
I AM always with you
And you are safe and secured in My love
I AM the GREAT I AM

"And God said unto Moses, I AM THAT I AM."
Exodus 3:14A

"Jesus said unto them, Verily, Verily, I say unto you,
before Abraham was, I AM."
John 8:58

A Heavenly Reminder (part 5)
Life Abundantly

I was talking to God this morning and asked Him,
"Lord, what would you like for me to share with
Your daughters/my sisters God?"
And in that still small voice, He replied
"Tell My daughters that _'the enemy comes to steal,_
kill, and destroy-but I AM come that they may have
life, but that they may have life ABUNDANTLY.'"
John 10:10

So, sis, are you just going through the motions of
life and barely existing? Or are you truly living in
the OVERFLOW and ABUNDANCE that comes
from Yeshua? Have you been dwelling in the valley
of dry bones, running on empty, or are you seeking
the milk and honey of the promised land?

Sometimes we have to take an internal inventory sis
and recognize and be real about our weaknesses and
when we're just exhausted and struggling. Not just
a physical exhaustion and struggle, but a mental,
emotional and spiritual one as well. From the
moment that we wake up, till we lay our heads
down at night, the enemy finds ways to get to us.
Has your joy been stolen lately? Has your peace
gone missing? When's the last time you truly smiled
and laughed carelessly? These are the gifts that our

Abba Father gives to you, so don't let the enemy rob them from you. When you're too tired to go on, God will carry you. Honor your body sis and rest (after all, God rested on the seventh day). He didn't create us to constantly be involved in something all of the time. He did create us to stay in communion and fellowship with Him. Find time this week or weekend to clear your schedule, clear your mind, and just sit at our Saviors feet. Find time to let Him love on you and let Him remind you of who you are in Him. He is still writing your story sis, stop letting others steal the pen.

Let's get to a place to where we're not just merely going through the motions and running on empty but truly living life in the OVERFLOW and ABUNDANCE like He has always intended for us to sis. Let's honor Him with our time and our lives and just watch as those things that once were missing…that the enemy once killed (peace, joy, a sound mind, comfort, strength, confidence, etc.) comes back to life and returns to you again.

Something Beautiful

Hey sis,

There's something BEAUTIFUL that God want to BIRTH in you. But just like any birth, there's going to be pain. There's going to be pain when it's time to push. There's going to be pain as those who you thought were for you is removed from your life. God has to remove them because they cannot see the importance and blessing and the weight of what you're carrying.

They say that they support you publicly but have disdain for you privately. So, God has to physically remove those who stand in the way spiritually. There's going to be pain as you face trials that come unexpectedly, as God carries you from this old version to preparing the new version (you cannot put old wine into a new wineskin), and things start to break off and fall away.

Hey sis,

Now is not the time to look back and long for who you thought would be there, what you thought it should look like or even how you thought this season of your life should be handled. God is ordering your steps sis and paving out the groundwork. He is preparing the table as well as the room for this spiritual birth to take place. He knows that it has to be a SAFE environment, a SECURE environment. An environment in which you are surrounded by other believers that are glued in to Him. And only those who are for you will have a place at this table. Only those who will hold your hand as you push, who will speak life in you, who will play a role in this birthing will be by your side. He is making your enemies your footstool.

So, trust the process sis and as you feel the pressure and weight of what you're carrying, allow it to draw you closer to Him. Allow it to be a reminder to keep your eyes on our Savior. Allow it to be a reminder that you have been set apart for such a time as this and the battlefield is messy but stand sis STAND!

There's something BEAUTIFUL that God wants to BIRTH in you.
And it's worth the pain, the tears, the heartaches, the separation, it's worth everything.

Cause with this BIRTH,
Comes an elevation.

With this BIRTH,
Comes a separation.

With this BIRTH,
Comes a sanctification.

With this BIRTH,
Comes a deeper calling, your true identity, armor to stand on this spiritual battleground and the authority to go into the enemy's camp and take back what was stolen.

So, RISE WARRIOR.
RISE.

There's something BEAUTIFUL that God wants to BIRTH in you.

Kingdom Anointing

You've got that kingdom anointing upon you sis
That's why they can't figure you out
So, talk kingdom
Walk kingdom
Think kingdom
Act kingdom
Cause you are beauty from ashes
You are the head and not the tail
You are the one whom the Lion of Judah rejoices in
You are His
You are
A kingdom girl.

You've got that kingdom anointing upon you sis
That's why your path has always looked different
That's how you've been able to forgive where
others couldn't forgive
Show grace where others haven't been able to
That is why you're still standing
After all that life has thrown at you
You are
A kingdom girl.

You've got that kingdom anointing upon you sis
That's why some don't stay around you long
Your light would expose their darkness

That's why the enemy has used others to manipulate
You, control you, use and reject you
Cause he knows what your destiny looks like
And he desires to distract, delay and discourage you
From getting there
So, stand from that anointing sis
Speak from that anointing sis
And fight from that anointing sis
You are
A kingdom girl
With a kingdom anointing.

Over looked by several
But seen by God
Dismissed by most
But held by God
Rejected by the "popular"
But accepted by the spiritual
That is why you've never been impressed
By the material
That is why you don't get caught up in silly games
You were birth with a desire to see
What others can't see
To understand where others are quick to judge
And to stay where most would leave
You were birth with a purpose
And destiny is within your bones
You are a kingdom girl
With a kingdom anointing.

Where are You?

Where are you?
I've prepared a table for you, but you've been
Sitting at everyone else's table but mine.
Where are you?
You've kept up with your social media notifications
And followings throughout the day,.
But scarcely checked in with Me.
Where are you?
You've talked to your coworker, your parent,
And your friend about that problem,
But have yet to talk to Me.
Where are you?
You picked up your Bible, but your phone rang
So, you sat it back down and it's been there all day.
Where are you?
For I never walk away from you,
But you've allowed the busyness of life to stray
And distract you from truly dwelling
In My presence.
So, where are you?
My Beloved, you've got to push through
The commitments, the obligations,
And seek Me first.
I AM the source that will get you through the day.
I AM the well that will never run dry.
I AM your hiding place, your shelter,
And your way maker.

I AM patiently waiting for you to call out
To My beloved.
My heart rejoices when you speak My name.
Where are you?
It's time to return to your first love.
Remember the enemy wants your mind on anything,
But me and your eyes on anything but the Bible
And your words full of worry more so than worship.
Where are you?
Just take a deep breath and fall into Me.
My arms are full of grace, mercy, and love.
Draw near to Me, and I, the Lord
Will draw near to you.
Where are you?
Come home to Me, My child.

Spiritually Naked

Don't go through life spiritually naked!

- You would never go out in public with no clothes on
- You would never go to work before being dressed
- You would never go to that meeting or event without the proper attire
- You would never have your friends/family over without some form of clothing on
- There are even places of business that will say, "no shoes, no shirts=no service"

Why not?

- To be naked is to be vulnerable
- To be naked would lead to some form of being uncomfortable (within yourself and those around you)
- To be naked would lead to being talked about, frowned upon, and judged
- Would lead to exposure to the elements
- No hiding or rather no covering
- No form of protection

Just as we wouldn't walk out that door, have friends over nor attend any events/ appointments without first being properly prepared to face each thing, it's equally as important that you don't go through your day naked spiritually. How are you covering/dressing yourself spiritually daily?

As you go about your day, ask yourself:

- Am I covered spiritually?
- What areas of my life have I left exposed for the enemy to get to?
- Have I taken the time to get dressed spiritually? Of course, there's a million things to do throughout the day, but don't let it deter you from the most important thing you should be doing (praying, worshipping, Bible time).

The enemy is always battle ready; You should be too sis (armor of God).

Biblical References:

Luke 10:38-42

Martha was consumed by busyness, Mary chose stillness.

Ephesians 6:11-17

The days are wicked, dress appropriately.

2nd Corinthians 5:1-4

We are clothed from heaven.

Is He (Welcomed in Your Home)

When you have a guest, you go out of your way to make them feel welcome in your home. You find out what foods they like as well as their preferred drinks. If you're a pet owner, you may even ask them if they are for or against pets. From there, you ask/ figure out a date and time that is most convenient for them to come over. When that day arrives, you make sure your home is prepared and cleaned for their arrival.

A lot of us are praying and asking for God's holy presence to dwell within our homes. But what are we doing to make Him feel welcomed? Not just our physical homes, but our spiritual homes as well. Are your words, thoughts, as well as actions and reactions cultivating an environment in which He feels welcome to dwell in?

"For I AM the Lord your God: ye shall therefore sanctify yourselves, and ye shall be holy; for I AM holy."
                    Leviticus 11:44

"Behold, I stand at the door and knock. If anyone hears My voice and opens the door, I will come in to him and dine with him and he with Me."
                    Revelation 3:20

By Faith

Now faith is the substance of things hoped for, the evidence of things not seen.

How would you describe faith? How does the world's definition of faith differ from that of the Bible? How does Jesus view your faith?

Every day we put our faith in something. When we lay our head down to sleep at night, we have faith that we will wake in the morning. When we order or door dash fast food/groceries, we have faith that everything that we order will arrive. When you step on a plane, you have faith that you'll make it to your destination. When we drop our kids off to the sitters or day care, we have faith that they will be taken care of. Will add one more that I heard from church-when you're driving and your light is green, you have faith that the other cars will stop that have the red light.

Hebrews chapter eleven consists of forty verses-fourteen of those starting with the words, *"by faith"* and *"through faith."* If your faith was something that could be seen with the physical eye, would it show? Does your faith sound like a new born kitten or does it roar like a lion standing on a mountain top? Our faith is something that we carry internally, but how do we show it (as well as share it)

126

externally? We live in a world in which people put their faith in almost anything. For example, growing up I had a rabbit's foot keychain that I kept in my pocket, believing that it would bring me luck. What's really popular now sadly even among Christians are stones and crystals. By the way-this is new age. I had to explain to another sister in Christ why we should not use sage to "clean" our home. We live in a world where people are so quick to rely on horoscopes, tarot cards (all new age and all part of my former life before coming to Christ) even psychics and mediums, yet will so quickly doubt or deny the word of God. When we place our faith in Jesus, why would we need to place our trust/faith in anything else? It would be like me carrying that rabbit foot keychain around today-it's like telling God, "I'm going to pray for xyz God, but just in case, here's my plan B."

To have a plan B is to tell God that we don't trust Him nor have full faith that He will answer that prayer. Now let me add, God's way is not our ways nor His thoughts our thoughts (*Isaiah 55:8-9*), so it's always in His timing and in His way. It may not look how you thought it would look. I can speak on this personally. I worked in retail for several years and finally landed an interview with a hospital. I was beyond thrill at the time. The actual interview went great, the conversation flowed easily, and we ended up even having some laughs together. I walked out of that room with my head held high so confident that I would be chosen for the job. Fast forward to two or three days later, I got a call from the lady that interviewed me. My heart was crushed when I was informed that they choose to go with someone else. I remember being upset and even sad for weeks over this-to the point, that I called them back and asked why I didn't get it (emotions out of control/leaning on my own understanding.) I shared this experience with one of my coworkers. Six months later, I got the news that that area of the hospital had closed down. I updated my coworker with the news and her response to me was, "see how God was looking out for you." I couldn't give her a response. I had let my feelings block my faith. And I had allowed what I thought was best for me to become more important than what God wanted for me-as a matter of fact, I don't even recall asking God if I should have applied for that position. Even with my lack of faith, God still looked out for me.

When Jesus called Peter out of the boat and to walk on water, as long as Peter kept his eyes on Jesus-he was fine. It took faith just to even get out of the boat. When Peter took his eyes off of Jesus and noticed the storm all around, that's when he started to drown-fear took over and when fear takes over, it pushes faith to the side, and we begin to sink. What is causing you to sink beneath the surface? Is it doubt, anxiety, shame, guilt? All of those will way you down.

When you're unsure about a situation or a decision that you have to make, don't rely on what you can see, taste, touch, and feel. Remember God sees what we can't see, and He knows what we may not know in that moment. Where we are limited to one day at a time-He sees it all-He's not bound by time. It's not always easy to do-but I am so grateful that we can cry out, "Lord, I believe-help thou my unbelief."

Mark 9:24

"For what saith the scripture? Abraham believe God, and it was counted unto him for righteousness."
Romans 4:3

"When Jesus saw their faith, He said unto the sick of the palsy, "Son, thy sins be forgiven thee."
Mark 2:5

"And He said unto her, 'Daughter, they faith hath made thee whole; go in peace and be whole of thy plague.'"
Mark 5:34

The Right Voice but Wrong Direction

1ˢᵗ Samuel 3:4-10

"That the Lord called Samuel; and he answered, Here am I. And he ran unto Eli, and said, Here am I; for thou calledst me. And he said, "I called not; lie down again. And he went and lay down. And the Lord called yet again, Samuel. And Samuel arose and went to Eli, and said, Here am I; for thou didst call me. And he answered, "I called not, my son; lie down again. Now Samuel did not yet know the Lord, neither was the word of the Lord yet revealed unto him. And the Lord called Samuel again the third time, And he arose and went to Eli, and said, Here am I; for thou didst call me. And Eli perceived that the Lord had called the child."

The Lord called Samuel, yet Samuel thought it was Eli calling him. God was speaking and Samuel heard correctly-the right voice, but he went in the wrong direction. How often can we say that of ourselves? How many times have we allowed a person, an opportunity, our flesh/emotions to pull us in a direction that God wasn't calling us to?
In the case of Samuel, Eli perceived that it was the Lord calling Samuel. Eli knew the Lord, which in itself was a blessing. How many times have we've gone in the wrong direction, strayed from God

cause we seek advice, happiness, and fulfillment from people, places, and situations that don't know God? How often do we allow these things to speak to us and guide us in place of God? We allow their voices, opinions, and advice to echo throughout our minds and subconsciously turn down God's voice. God has been calling you patiently and personally by name, but you've allowed the things of this world to get in the way. Too many voices drown out the voice of God.

We need to make sure we have Elis in our lives. An Eli is someone who knows and recognizes God's voice. An Eli will humbly step out of the way and tell us how to respond to God's calling. He won't be intimated nor threatened by the calling on your life but will encourage you to embrace it. An Eli is someone in whom God can trust in when He is calling, you'll be pointed in the right direction. Who is your Eli?

It's time that we stop allowing our flesh to guide us, the news scare us, social media distract us and others deter us. My dear sister, it's time that we respond to God such as Samuel and say, "speak, for thy servant hear." What or rather who is keeping you from clearly hearing God calling you? Who do you turn to when you feel His gentle nudge? There is so much that God has placed inside of you-don't allow how others perceive you (nor how you perceive yourself) to keep it in nor hidden.

Who is your Eli? If you haven't found the Eli in your life, I added this prayer for God to guide you so your paths will cross.

Remember, an Eli-walks with God, talks with God, recognizes His voice and is humble enough to step out of the way. Pray with me.

Father God,

I thank You so much for my sister who is reading this right now. Father God, just as You called to Samuel and Samuel had yet to recognize your voice-I pray that you will bring an Eli into her life Lord. Someone who knows you, has been walking with You Lord and seeks You on all things God. I pray dear Lord that you give this person eyes to see the work that You are doing within my sister and ears to hear when You are calling her Father. Father God, I thank You for the Elis. Pleas bless them both dear Lord, lead and guide them and may they always be in tune with Your voice.

In Jesus name,

Amen

Be Not Deceived

Satan already knows that he is defeated and will be thrown into the lake of fire for all eternity. His main goal is to take as many souls with him as possible. DO NOT BE DECIEVED! DO NOT LOVE THE THINGS OF THIS WORLD! For all the things that he's telling you to love, that it's okay to love, and that it's acceptable to love is only to pull you from God's truth and to get you off the straight and narrow path. DO NOT BE DECIEVED! FOR HE IS A LIAR AND THE TRUTH IS NOT IN HIM! Don't take my word for it, open up your Bible and read God's truth on it. Don't wait until it's too late, give your life to Jesus today. Forsake this world and run to Jesus!

"In whom the god of this world (satan) hath BLINEDED the minds of them which believe not, lest the light of the glorious gospel of Christ, who is the image of God, should shine unto them."
2nd Corinthians 4:4

"And the devil that DECEIVED them was cast into the lake of fire and brimstone, where the beast and false prophet are & shall be tormented day and night for ever and ever."
Revelation 20:10

"Ye adulterer and adulteresses, know ye not that friendship of this world id enmity with God? Whosoever therefore will be a friend of this world is an enemy to God."

James 4:4

"Know ye not that the UNRIGHTEOUS shall not inherit the kingdom of God? BE NOT DECIEVED, neither fornicators, nor idolaters, nor adulterers, or effeminate, nor abusers of themselves with mankind, nor thieves, nor covetous, nor drunkards, nor revilers, nor extortioners, shall inherit the kingdom of God."

1st Corinthians 9:10

I Miss You

♥ I MISS YOU

I watch as you go about your day talking to
everyone else and oh, how I long for you to talk to
Me. It grieves My heart when I see the one whom I
fearfully and wonderfully made worry about the
physical things that are spiritually not good for you.
Just as a mother holds her child's hands so that the
child doesn't run into the road, I-your heavenly
Father wants to hold your hand to save you from the
impact of the blow that you did not see coming. But
you must let Me in, you must get to a place of
vulnerability with Me. I know what you stand in
need of before you ask, I knitted and formed you in
your mother's womb. I know you on a level that
others can't grasp, so won't you trust the One who
created and truly cares for you?

♥ I MISS YOU

So, please step away from all the noise from time to
time. This world is set up to keep you busy, keep
you distracted, keep you engaged, keep you
overwhelmed. But I am asking beloved, that you
please surrender to the stillness of Me. That you'll
disengage with the world in order to engage with
Me. That instead of running to your friends first for

advice, run to Me. Call out Abba Father and I will answer. I AM always speaking, my beautiful one, but you must get close and be still to hear.

♥ I MISS YOU
Won't you come away with Me?
♥ I MISS YOU
-God

Let There Be Light

And God said, let there be light; and there was light. And God SAW the light, that it was good. And God DIVIDED the light from the darkness.

God CREATED light
God SAW that the light was good
God DIVIDED the light from darkness

When we become a new creation in Christ, His light falls upon us. When we decide to walk with our King, we can no longer walk with darkness. God is the one who creates, sees, and divides the light from darkness (it's all spiritual). Our natural instinct...our sinful nature aka our flesh (which doesn't care about where we spend eternity cause it's not going with us), desires those things and works of darkness. We cannot escape nor walk away from the darkness on our own (for the flesh and spirit are constantly at war with each other). Hence, it takes our heavenly Father who created us and sees us to divide us from that darkness, that sinful nature, and our flesh. The first thing that God did when He created, saw the light, and saw that it was good was divide it from the darkness (the bad). *Deuteronomy 14:2* tells us that we have been set apart. When you're on the path for Christ, there are certain places that you can no longer go. When you're standing for Christ, there will be people that will no longer stand with you. See, the darkness cannot comprehend the light. That is why, when you speak on the things of God, some people don't understand, nor will they get your passion and zeal for the Lord. How can we not be passionate about and have zeal for the One who laid down His life while we were still yet sinners?

You will know other light bearers. They will naturally gravitate towards your light. You will know those that are still in darkness when offense comes to them, discord, and anger. You will know them by their fruits. Not everyone who has ears will hear what thus the Lord has to say. My sister do not be sad for or worry about the things, the places, and the people God separates you from when He allows His light to fall upon you. You are being renewed by His mercy and grace each day, transformed, and prepared to carry His anointing to hear so clearly from Him. So, let the former things stay in Egypt, lace up your shoes sis, and walk the path to the land overflowing with milk and honey. Our Father is light, so let the world see His light within you. Our Father is love, so be an example of His love. Do not mourn the division sis but rather rejoice in what/who/where He is taking you to.

"And the light shineth in darkness; and the darkness comprehended it not."
John 1:5

"Ye are the light of the world. A city that is set on a hill cannot be hid. Neither do men light a candle, and put it under a bushel, but on a candlestick and it giveth light unto all that are in the house. Let your light so shine before men, that they may see your good works, and glorify your Father which is in heaven."

Matthew 5:14-16

"Then spake Jesus again saying unto them, I am the light of the world; he that followeth after Me shall not walk in darkness, but shall have the light of life."

John 8:12

"And the light shineth in darkness, and the darkness comrprehened it not."

John 1:5

"For the flesh lusteth against the spirit, and the spirit against the flesh; and these are contrary the one to the other: so that ye cannot do the things that ye would. But if ye be led of the spirit, ye are not under the law. Now the works of the flesh are manifest, which are these; adultery, fornication, uncleanness, lasciviousness, idolatry, witchcraft, hatred, variance, emulations, wrath, strife, seditions, heresies, envying, murders, drunkenness, revellings, and such like." Galatians 5:17-2

If You're Going To

If you're going to WALK,
Then walk in the anointing that is over your life.
Walk in the authority that is freely given as a believer in Christ.
Walk in the confidence that YOU ARE the daughter of the ONE TRUE KING, knowing and trusting that no weapon formed against you will prosper.

If you're going to TALK,
Then talk about how God made a way when there was no way.
Talk about the goodness of God.
Talk in such a way that people are drawn to you, uplifted by you, and encouraged by your words.

If you're going to LISTEN,
Then listen to the still small voice of Jehovah.
Then listen to those that speak of your future, not about your past.
Listen to those that can see how God has changed you and believe in the calling that's on your life.

And when you get DRESS,
Be sure that you're dressed in the full armor of God.
Be sure that you've covered your day, your mind, and your heart in prayers.
Be sure to cover yourself in the mercy and goodness of God.

And when you REST,
Be sure to rest in His promises.
Be sure to lean back and cozy up to Jesus.
Be sure to silence the world and be still with the One who created the world.
Rest in His goodness, rest in His peace, Rest in His glory, and rest in Him.

And when you REFLECT,
Reflect on how God chased after you was you walked away.
Reflect on all the times that He made a way.
Reflect on the trials that you walked through in which He held your hand.
Reflect on His goodness, faithfulness and steadfast love.
Reflect on how He loved you even when you weren't loving Him.

And when you WORSHIP,
Worship the GREAT I AM for everything that He is and for everything that you are in Him.
Worship Him for changing you from the inside out, for taking away that heart of stone, and giving you a heart of flesh.
Worship Him for picking you up in the middle of your mess, in the middle of your brokenness, and doubt.
Worship Him for giving you a new name and beauty for ashes.
Worship Him, for He is worthy of all the praise.
Worship Him as you walk.
Worship Him as you talk.
Worship Him as you listen.

Worship Him as you dress.
Worship Him as you rest.
Worship Him as you reflect.
Worship Him.
Always.

Have You Tried Jesus?

So, you've been seeking a safe place.
Have you tried the arms of Jesus?
So, you've been looking for a love that will never fail you.
Have you tried the love of Jesus?
So, you've been wanting promises that will never fail.
Have you read about and tried the promises of Jesus?
So, you're tired of holding on to your hurts, guilts, and shames.
Have you tried the forgiveness of Jesus?
Tired of people that misunderstands you?
Have you tried the One whom created you?
So, you're tired of the shackles, demands, and labels of this world.
Have you tried the freedom found in Jesus?
So, you're overwhelmed by the confusion and chaos.
Have you found the peace and clarity in Jesus?
Whatever it is that you're going through, regardless of the shame and dirt thrown at you,
Have you tried the One who was nailed to the cross to redeem you?
I know the One who can wash and make you whole.
I know the One that still sets the captives free.
I know the One whose arms are opened wide.

Have you tried the One who holds your true
identity?
Jesus.
His name is Jesus.
Have you tried my Jesus?

*"For God so loved the world, that He gave His only
begotten Son, that whosever believes in Him should
not perish but have eternal life."*
                    John 3:16

*"For I am persuaded that neither death, nor life,
nor angels, nor principalities, nor powers, nor
things present, nor things to come, nor height, nor
depth, nor any other creature shall be able to
separate us from the love of God, which is in Christ
Jesus our Lord."*
                    Romans 8:38-39

*"A man that hath friends must shew himself
friendly: and there is a friend that sticketh closer
than a brother."*
                    Proverbs 18:24

Hey Sis

Hey sis
If you've been feeling weary,
This is your sign to keep going.
Hey sis
If you've been feeling overwhelmed this is
Your reminder to not throw in the towel just yet.
Hey sis
If you've been in a storm,
This is your reminder that storms don't last.
Hey sis
Don't worry about who's talking about you
And spreading rumors about you.
You know your truth (which is what God says about
you), so stand in it and let your character speak for
you (remember, the truth is always quiet and can
stand alone, lies area always loud and seeks an
audience).
Hey sis
Don't come into agreement with what the enemy
Is whispering in your ear.
He is the father of all lies and the truth isn't in him.
Hey sis
You've come too far to look back now.
Hey sis
You will rejoice in the same places
That once held your tears.

Hey sis

Joy is your portion. Peace is your portion.

Contentment too.

Hey sis

You are worthy of stability and clarity.

Don't let the enemy confuse you.

Hey sis

You are amazing.

You are beautiful and there is no one like you.

So, keep going.

One day at a time, one task at a time.

Hey sis

You've got this! And I am cheering for you.

Completely

If you're going to fall into His arms, then fall into
His arms completely.

Completely broken.
Completely undone.
Completely vulnerable.
Completely flawed.
Completely with your struggles.
Completely with your tears.
Completely with your mistakes.
Completely put your heart in His hands.
He is the One who knows how to mend it
Back to health, to life, to joy, to completeness
He is the One who formed and fashioned

Your heart after all. ♥

He is the One who loves you unconditionally
And oh, so faithfully.
He will lift you up and never let you down.
It is not too late to lift your eyes up to the hills
From whence our help comes from.
He is waiting.
Faithfully
Anxiously
Patiently
For you to call upon His name.
For you to allow Him into your heart.
His arms are opened.

His eyes full of warmth.
He is smiling at you.
You are on His mind.
So, won't you
Completely
Turn to Him.
Run to Him.
Talk to Him.
Surrender to Him.
Trust Him.
He is waiting.
Just for you.

The Refining Process

Changes will come sis.

There will be places you no longer wish to go, environments you no longer desire to dwell in, and situations you no longer wish to be a part of. As a result of that, there will be people left behind (not saying for bad reasons or that they are bad people) just that God may not desire for them to go into the season where He is calling you into (the caterpillar is often alone during the process of becoming a butterfly).

It's called the refining process.

It's what happens when we, the clay, allow the Potter to mold us in His hands (*Isaiah 64:8*) with the goal to become more like Him.

Where God is calling you spiritually is worth everything He's asking and showing you to leave behind physically. He never takes away without replacing in order to get down to the very essence of who and what He is calling you to be...that new creation in Christ (*2nd Corinthians 5:17*). There has to be a shedding and a separation of the old.

Do not mourn the former things left behind sis. Instead, rejoice in the new. Old keys don't unlock new doors, and He is calling you to go deeper with Him, and spend more time with Him.

And of course, what God has for you, the enemy wants to steal from you. So, stand guarded and planted in the word. Don't allow the opinions of others to take away from what God is telling you. This is your spiritual journey sis, between you and Him; not everyone will understand and it's okay. They didn't understand Jesus either. Keep your eyes focused on Him, continue to let Him do a good work in you (*Philippians 1:6*), and clothe yourself oh so graciously in your identity in Him…attire which consist of beauty for ashes, grace and mercy, forgiveness, and unfailing love. Wear it so much so that others desire to clothe themselves in the beauty and promises of God's love and truth.

Let There Be Light

- & God **SAID,** let there be light; & there was light.
- & God **SAW** the light, that it was good.
- & God **DIVIDED** the light from the darkness. (*Genesis 1:3-5*)

- God **CREATED** light
- God **SAW** that the light was good
- God **DIVIDED** the light from darkness

When we become a new creation in Christ, His light falls upon us. When we decide to walk with our King, we can no longer walk with darkness. God is the one who creates, sees, and divides the light from darkness (it's all spiritual). Our natural instinct, our sinful nature/ our flesh (which doesn't care where we spend eternity cause it's not going with us) desires those things and works of darkness. We cannot escape nor walk away from the darkness on our own (for the flesh and the spirit are constantly at war with each other according to *Galatians 5:17*). Hence, it takes our heavenly Father who created us and sees us to divide us from the darkness, from that sin that we cling to, the mindset, and the ways that have kept us in chains for far too long. The first thing God did when He created and saw the light and saw that it was good was divide it from darkness (the bad). *Deuteronomy 14:2* tells us that we have been set apart. When you're on the path with Christ, there are certain places that you can no longer go. When you're standing for Christ, there will be people that will no longer stand with you. See, the darkness cannot comprehend the light (*John 1:5*) that's why when you speak on the things of God, some people won't understand nor will they get your passion and zeal for the Lord. How can we not be passionate about and have zeal for the One who laid down His life while yet we were still sinners (*Romans 5:8*)? You will know other light bearers cause they will naturally gravitate towards your light. You will know those that are still in the darkness when offense comes to them, discord, and anger. You will know them by their fruits (*Matthew 7:15-20*). Not everyone who has ears will hear what thus the Lord has to say. My sister, do not be sad for or worry about the things, the places, and the people God separates you from when He allows His light to fall upon you. You are being renewed by His mercy and grace each day, transformed, and prepare to carry His anointing and to hear so clearly from Him. So, let the former things stay in Egypt, lace up your shoes sis, and walk the path to the land overflowing with milk and honey. Our Father is light, so let the world see His light through you. Our Father is love, so be an example of His love. Do not mourn the division sis, but rather rejoice in the what, the who, and the where He is taking you.

"Ye are the light of the world. A city that is set on a hill cannot be hid. Neither do men light a candle and put it under a bushel, but on a candlestick and it giveth light unto all that are in the house. Let your light so shine before men, that they may see your good wors, and glorify your Father which is in heaven."
Matthew 5:14-16

"Then spake Jesus again saying unto them, I am the light of the world; he that followeth after Me shall not walk in darkness, but shall have the light of life."
John 8:12

"And the light shineth in darkness, and the darkness comprehended it not."
John 1:5

"Now the works of the flesh are manifest, which are these, adultery, fornication, uncleanness, lasciviousness, idolatry, witchcraft, hatred, variance, emulations, wrath, strife, seditions, heresies, envyings, murders, drunkenness, revellings, and such like; of the which I tell you before, as I have also told you in time past, that they

which do such things shall not inherit the kingdom of God
But the fruit of the Spirit is love, joy, peace, longsuffering, gentleness, goodness, faith, meekness, temperance, against such there is no law."

Galatians 5:19-23

Phone Call with God

Caller: God, are you there? I know it's been awhile since I've called out to you and even longer that I've trusted You. Despite running to everyone and trying everything else, I still feel empty and broken. I've tried it all, but You Lord. But here I am now, God. I have no place left to go. Is it too late for me? I pray that I'm not too dirty to call out to You.

God: My precious Child, I have always been here. I am a good, good Father as well as the perfect gentleman-I only come in as far as you'll let me. Take heart, my beautiful one, every tear that you have ever cried I hold on My hands. My faithfulness is steadfast and you will always find Me when you seek Me with your whole heart.

Caller: Heavenly Father, I'm tired of crying.

God: Weeping may endure for a night, but joy comes in the morning.
Psalm 30:5B

Caller: I'm going through tough times my Father.

God: My cherished one, count it all joy when you fall into various trials knowing that the testing of your faith produces patience.

James 1:2-3

Caller: My heart keeps getting broken Lord.

God: For by a sad countenance the heart is made better. The heart of the wise is in the house of the mourning.

Ecclesiastes 7:3-4

Caller: I feel ugly Lord.

God: My love, you are fearfully and wonderfully made.

Psalm 139:1-4

Caller: Society is so quick to judge and hurt me Lord.

God: My beautiful one, for man look at the outward appearance, but I look at the heart.

1st Samuel 16:7

Caller: Temptation is everywhere Lord and sometimes it calls my name.

God: But, I am faithful. I will not suffer you to be tempted above that ye are able, but with the temptation also make a way to escape, that ye may be able to bear it. The wages of sin is death; but the gift of God is eternal life through Jesus Christ our Lord.

1ˢᵗ Corinthians 10:13B & Romans 6:23

Caller: I'm exhausted all the time Lord. Sometimes, I just want to give up.

God: Come to Me all who labor and are heavy laden, and I will give you rest. Take My yoke upon you and learn from Me, for I am gentle and lowly in heart, and you will find rest for your souls. For My yoke is easy and My burden is light.

Matthew 11:28-30

Caller: Lord, my life isn't going how I thought it would go. I try to make things better, but they either stay the same or get worse. I try to clean up these messes only to end up in bigger messes God. What am I doing wrong Lord?

God: Beloved, trust in Me with all Your heart and lean not on your own understanding. For I know the thoughts (plans) that I think toward you, saith the Lord, thoughts of peace, and not of evil, to give you an unexpected end.

Proverbs 3:5 & Jeremiah 29:11

Caller: There's so much darkness in this world.

God: You are the light of the world. Let your light shine before men, that they may see your good works and glorify your Father in heaven.
Matthew 5:14a&16

Caller: I'm being pulled in so many different directions, Lord. So many people are speaking into my life.

God: My sheep hear of My voice, and I know them, and they follow Me.
John 10:27

Caller: Lord, I am afraid to take this journey with You, how do I know that I can trust You and that You'll see me through?

God: Before I formed you in the womb I knew you, I know the very number of hairs upon your head & beloved, I am not man that I should lie.
Jeremiah 1:5, Luke 12:7, Numbers 23:19

Caller: Whom am I to You, Lord?

God: You are the apple of My eye, My beautiful bride. The one whom I have set apart and called by name.
Psalm 17:8, Revelation 19:7-8

Caller: Okay God, I think I'm ready to let You in. How do we start?

God: If thou shalt confess with thy mouth the Lord Jesus, and shalt believe in thine heart that God hath raised Him from the dead, thou shalt be saved. Confess in your heart and you will be saved. Repent ye and believe in the gospel.
Romans 10:9 & Mark 1:15B

God: Daughter, welcome home.

Eternity

I care more about your soul and where you'll spend eternity more so than seeing you "live your best life" and doing what "makes you happy" (side note: we are called to be holy as He is holy). We weren't created to settle for the temporary pleasures and ways of this world. We are to be imitators of Christ, and we are called to pick up our cross daily and deny the flesh. So many people say that they know God and have their own relationship with Him. You cannot have a relationship with Christ on your terms. You've got to know and live by what thus says the Lord. The only way to get to God is through our Lord and Savior Jesus Christ. He literally gave His life for us. He tells us that if we love Him, we will keep His commandments. We can't pick and choose the ones we want to follow nor take them out of context to justify how we are living.

I am far from perfect, but my goal is to live a life that is pleasing to Him. to be convicted and corrected when I am wrong. To keep my feet on the straight and narrow path (for wide is the gate of destruction and many go there in) and to repent of my sins and flee from them. The enemy always tries to tempt us (that's his goal). The world tells us that if we don't go along to get along, then we are full of hate. If I'm full of hate, then I'd rather hate you to heaven than love you to hell.

Well, guess what? Jesus was counted out too and I'd rather be counted out with Jesus then counted in with the world. Every single person that God used in the Bible was counted out in some way or form. Joseph was counted out by his brothers, David was counted out by his dad, and the blind man was counted out (and kicked out of the city) after being healed by Jesus.

I may not know you and our paths may never cross while we are here on this side of the Earth, but I do know that you are someone that Jesus went to the cross for. I do know that He loves you with a love that no one and nothing in this world could ever compare. I do know that if you were to let Him in (truly let Him in) you would be filled with a peace unexplainable, joy incomparable, and He would show you who you were always meant to be. If you're looking to the world for answers, there's a very high chance that they are going to get it wrong. No one knows you like He knows you sis and He is waiting ever so patiently for you to run into His arms. So, please don't fall for the lies of the enemy, your flesh, nor your feelings. These things will cheat you out of eternity with your heavenly Father. This world is fading away every day and the trumpet will soon sound. Repent and give your life to Jesus today.

Spoiler alert 1: Satan doesn't care about you. He already knows where he is going, and his goal is to take as many souls with him as possible.

Spoiler alert 2: Your sin doesn't love you, and you don't have control over it. Surrender to Jesus and be free in His name.

Spoiler alert 3: Regardless of if you believe or not, every knee shall bow and tongue confess that Christ is Lord.

Spoiler alert 4: Disagreeing with a person doesn't mean the love isn't still there. We can agree to disagree and still be kind.

If you are unsure about where you will spend eternity, please reach out to someone that is biblically sound and walking with Christ fully. Ask them about Jesus and the gift of eternal salvation. If you've been mixing new age with Christianity, please repent and walk away from it. There's no such thing as good magic, white magic, sage, yoga, reiki, mediums, etc. Read what the Word of God says about all that and pray for understanding as well as clarity from God. Come out from among them and be ye separate.

Prayers

A Prayer for Your Work Week
Day 1

Abba Father,

I pray dear Lord for my sister that is reading this right now. I ask that You'll please go before her and stand behind her. Give her endurance and wisdom to handle every obstacle, decision, and situation that she will face this week Lord.

I pray dear Lord that when folks try to bring her down, she looks up to You. I pray that she walks in the favor and anointing upon her life.

I pray that when the world tries to tell her who she is, she hears Your still small voice speaking over her. Remind her, Father, that she is far above rubies, a chosen generation, and far more precious than silver and gold.

I pray dear Lord that when everything around her feels unsteady and shaking, You will fill her with Your peace and remind her that she is held by Daddy.

Lord, she is Your daughter. I ask that You hide her from every scheme, plot, and trap set up by the enemy. Allow her to see everything and everyone for what and who they truly area. Remind her that Your promises are yes and amen! Remind her that with You, she is more than a conqueror. Abba, we thank You for ordering our steps and being all that we need.

In Yeshua's name I pray,
Amen

Day 2

Abba Father,

I thank You Daddy for allowing us to see another day. I thank You Lord for giving my sister the strength and endurance to get through the beginning of her work week. Lord, just as You carried her through yesterday, I pray that You carry her today too. Please touch her mind dear Lord and help her to focus on one thing at a time. Remind her to not take on too much. Lord if she's feeling overburden, I pray that she leans on You. If she's feeling fatigued, I pray that she rests in You. Lord, You hold all things in Your hands and nothing ever comes as a surprise to You. Prepare her heart and her mind dear Lord for what may come that's unexpected. And when and if the unexpected comes Lord, I pray that You'll remind her that You're already there and more than willing to see her through. Lord, I thank You for being our peace. I thank You for being our comfort.

In Yeshua's name I pray,
Amen

Day 3

Abba Father,

I thank You Abba that Your daughter was born for such a time as this. I thank You Lord for all the times that You have carried her, held her, and healed her. I thank You dear Lord for all the times You've held her back from what/ who would have harmed her or took away from her. Lord, please give her eyes to see and ears to hear. Please remind her that when life gets heavy, she can hand the heaviness to You. I thank You Lord that Your shoulders are strong enough to carry it. Your hands are gentle enough to heal. Your eyes and voice lovingly are enough to correct Your child and bring her back to You.

Lord, please touch her mind right now. Give her the endurance and strength needed to get through the reminder of the week. Please blow on her a fresh wind that will revive her weariness Lord. Remind her to look up when it seems as though things are going down. Remind her Lord that she is an overcomer by the blood. I thank You Lord that You make all things new.

In Yeshua's name I pray,
Amen

Day 4

Abba Father,

I thank You dear Lord for my sister in Christ.
Father, I thank You for seeing her through every
obstacle and situation she has faced this week (both
at work as well as at home). Lord, I thank You that
You called her Your own long before the world had
the chance to call her anything else. Lord, I thank
You for blessing her. Thank You for giving her the
ability to work and thank You for being her
provider. I pray that she doesn't get caught up in the
stress and busyness of work. I pray that she listens
to her body when it's telling her that she needs a
break. Remind her dear Lord that she cannot pour
from an empty cup. May she be reminded that the
enemy will use those closest to her to get her off
course, discouraged, and off center. Remind her that
it's all spiritual and that You have promised to fight
her battles. I pray dear Lord that she leans into You
a little bit more as the work week comes to a close.
Lord, help her to be a good steward of her time and
all that You have blessed her with.

In Yeshua's name I pray,
Amen

Day 5

Abba Father,

Father God, thank You for seeing my sister through another work week. I thank You dear Lord, for the hedge of protection around her that's kept her safe. Father, as my sister prepares for a day off, I pray that she prepares to spend some time with You. Show her what truly matters Lord. May she enter into a <u>Mary moment</u>: Choosing that good part that *"will not be taken away from her" (Luke 10:41-42).*

I pray dear Lord that You will touch her heart and that she will come into a place of transparency and honesty with You, Lord. I pray that she shares not only the good parts of her life, but the bad and ugly as well Lord knowing and trusting that You can make it all beautiful. Father, please help to make her crooked paths straight. May she tune out every voice that would subtly lead her astray including her own when it's not lining up with Your word, Lord. Abba, please continue to order her steps and show her the way to go. May she not lean on her own understanding but in all her ways may she acknowledge You. I pray that she feels and experiences Your presence unlike before. Lord, show her exactly who You are in her life and just how much she means to You. Father God, help her to look forward when she is tempted to look back. When the enemy messes with her mind (bringing up who she used to be, what she used to do, and her past mistakes) remind her of the love You have for her God. Thank You, Lord, for being with her, guiding her, and calling her Your own. May she begin to see herself as you see her Lord. I pray dear Lord that she surrenders all to You as her walk with You deepens. Lead her besides still waters Abba. May she always hear Your still small voice. Thank You Abba for calling her Your own.

In Yeshua's name,
Amen

Marilyn's Hard Knock Life Lessons

Marilyn's Hard Knock Life Lessons

How God took me from victim to victory!

When God told me that it was time to share my testimony, how He delivered me from witchcraft was my main focus. In reflecting on my past and my life before I allowed Him in, I've come to realize that there is another part of the story that I've yet to fully share. Yes, a big part of who I used to be is messy, ugly, even painful to recall, but I thank God for saving me from the life that I thought I wanted. How do you know that your life has gone downhill when it's become your normal? How do you come to expect better treatment from others when the bare minimum is what you're used to? It's hard to believe that you're somebody when you're treated like no one.

My parents divorced while I was really young, so growing up I didn't have that example of what a healthy marriage looked like. Our emotions nor how to properly process them was never discussed. We never talked about serious things nor the hard things. I remember when my mom would get mad at my sister, she just wouldn't talk to her for a few days (and vice versa). I remember seeing them pass each other in the hallway without a word. I always thought that it was so silly, but I was a kid, so what did I know? I learned to keep a lot on the inside and to suffer in silence. I guess because I was going to school and making good to decent grades, I was deemed to be "okay" or "just fine." That couldn't have been further from the truth. I would have thoughts of running away from home and harming myself. And when the pain became too much on the inside, I would scratch and scratch my wrists (I always had long nails) and wouldn't stop until the skin broke and/ or I was bleeding. I can still recall to this day how I couldn't feel the pain physically from my nails. I was going through life numb and had normalized it. I truly believe that people do the best that they can or know how to, so I don't blame my parents nor my upbringing at all. If anything, I've learned to be okay with my thoughts and to see the good in everything.

In elementary school one day, we had an assignment to write about our favorite holiday. That's when my first poem was written, and from there, writing became a form of therapy for me. Allowing me to unlock all the things that I had caged within. Writing became my lifeline.

It wasn't until I got my first job while in high school that I got a small taste of freedom (I wasn't given much wiggle room while in school). With the job came my first vehicle. Needless to say, I went through a reckless phase. I placed my identity in the world and allowed the people around me to dictate my happiness. This ended up with me meeting someone, becoming serious, and finding out that I was pregnant. We eventually got our own place and then married (in that order: I wasn't walking with God back then).

We had been together for a long time that people would constantly ask us "when are y'all getting married?" I'll pause here just to say, be mindful of who is in your ear and take everything to God. He will never lead you astray. I can only speak for myself, so I guess it felt like the right thing to do. However, looking back, we were both still very young and really didn't fully understand the roles and responsibilities that come from marriage nor what it really means to be husband and wife.

It started with small arguments (even before we moved in together). It then progressed to getting called out of my name and being put down verbally. The physical violence was at a minimum, but sometimes words hurt worse. Looking back, there were so many red flags, but I stayed cause I thought that was what I was supposed to do. I had no one that I could truly talk to. Since we both came from divorced parents, it was my desire to give my son a life that I never had (both parents in the house).

Living together, I should have finally felt free to raise our little family, but it felt like the freedom as well as the life was being squeezed out of me with every accusation and each blow that I endured. We would have our good moments, but they would be short lived and followed by a fight. And because I didn't know myself/ my identity nor knew God, my purpose was to please my husband.

I would change the way I looked. A few times, I got my hair cut to try to please him. I literally would have thoughts such as "if I did this or did that, then he'll love me." I entertained conversations that no married couple should entertain and went to places that gratify the flesh. All of this was under the guise of wanting to make him happy. I miscarried twice and was told that it was my fault. It didn't matter what I tried to do. It was never right. On the outside, we were the perfect couple, but so much was falling apart on the inside.

Then out of the blue one day, God used my older brother to invite us to church. We eventually said yes, and I am so glad that I did cause Jesus was waiting for me there. My son and I stayed in church. It became such a vital part of our life and helped us to grow in our relationship together. I threw away all my occult belongings, dropped to me knees, and asked God to forgive me. You see, God found me even when I wasn't looking for Him. God started to open my eyes to the reality of how I was living as well as the marriage that I was in. He kept whispering to me that this wasn't His idea of marriage. I started to find myself in church more as God allowed spirit filled ladies to come into my life and with every encounter I had with Him as I prayed and read my Bible.

And one day, I realized that I was tired of fighting. I came to the conclusion that they didn't amount to anything. So, when the fights/ anger would come, I wouldn't respond, or I would say something positive. This just made things worse for a while, but I kept on keeping on. Now, my eyes were focused on Jesus. I could feel that I was changing and that my confidence was coming back.

God truly was taking my heart of stone and giving me a heart of flesh. Since God had forgiven me, I was willing to forgive him. I knew that we couldn't keep going the way that we had been. I held on for an extra three months by praying and talking to God daily about what's next. Even though I was starting to walk with Christ, I knew that if I continued to stay within that marriage, I would believe that I was everything that he was speaking over me.

Now, I came into this marriage with my own baggage as well and I allowed some things in that shouldn't have been, but with Jesus, I was ready to change. I was looking forward to and excited about a fresh start in which we treated one another with honor and respect and showed our son what a Godly marriage looked like. However, I was the only one that wanted to take it there. Yes, I do believe that love is worth fighting for, but when you're the only one fighting, you eventually become exhausted and have no fight left in you.

Needless to say, after a lot of prayer and endless tears, I decided to move out. My son and I lived with my sister for a while (he was still little). It was me and him and the majority of our belongings in my old room. We eventually got our own place not too far from family, but we were starting over with a hand me down bed and a clear tote only full of odd and end things that I could afford at the time. We literally were starting over from scratch.

Once again, I found myself back at that place of just being numb. I was hurting so much on the inside that I was barely functioning throughout the day. I wanted the fairy tale cause that's what they sell us in the movies right? I wanted the one marriage and the "happily ever after." And I had that mindset of if I change myself then he'll love me and be loyal to me as well. I've come to realize that the "love" that they show us on TV and sing about isn't the love of Christ. So here I was starting over again. And looking back, I realized that I had never asked God if this was the person He had for me, nor if this was the way that I should go. I was leaning on self and my own understanding. I was doing things the way the world told us to do them-thinking that that would make me happy.

I was able to slowly furnish our home. I purchased my son his own bed (which he was super grateful for) and made a simple living for us. I was going through the divorce process during this time. I recall sitting on the couch one day as I was reflecting on my life/marriage and seeing in my mind's eye a fork in the road with me standing there. I remember thinking "I have two choices". I could go one way and become a victim and allow what I've been through as well as the abuse to follow and define me…or I could go the other way and become victorious by using this as an opportunity for a fresh start and making a new life for myself and my son. I chose to be victorious.

It was a long and painful process. I mourned for the life that I thought I wanted. I mourned for the marriage that we could have had. I mourned the fact that my son was going to be raised in a broken home. My tears could have filled an ocean. But even through the mourning, I kept pressing on. Even through the mourning, God kept showing up. Even through the mourning, the days became brighter and my heart lighter. I was starting to see myself as His.

Why am I sharing this part of my life with you? Because if the pain that I've endured can save one person from suffering, then it was well worth it. Because now that I'm older and have been walking with Christ a little bit longer, my perspective on so many things have changed. He's given me wisdom (not to say that I still don't have moments of being foolish sometimes) and growth. I share for the young ladies out there that are being told that they are only worth their body, that it's okay to show some skin (God honors modesty), and that your value is only found in what a guy tells you or how they treat you. I share for the youth and teens out there that have not been told who they are and who are looking for fulfilment in all the wrong things.

I've tried all that the world has to offer, and it always left me empty. I share cause I've learned that a healthy relationship requires so much more than love. It also requires mutual respect, understanding and compromise. Loyalty is so rare these days but just look at how loyal God has been to us. I share cause I was the girl who wanted to be loved and accepted so badly that I was willing to change everything about myself. Sis, you'll never have to compromise your values and integrity for someone that is meant for you. I share cause struggles and heartaches are a part of life, but for some reason, having emotions is frowned upon in today's society.

I thank God for my journey cause it's made me who I am today. I thank Him for every tear that I've cried and hard decision that I've had to make. Through it all, He has never left my side. My joy and happiness come from Him now. And when it comes from God, the world can't take it away. If you are feeling unseen, just know that you are seen by God. If you are feeling unloved, you are tremendously loved by God. You are just one prayer away from getting to know Him. As God's daughters, we are His heart outside of His chest (credit to Trevor Short).

I pray that this is your reminder that you are loved, treasured, and held by Him. You were not created to live a mediocre life or to just go through the motions. You are called to do great things for His glory. You are made in His image and the apple of His eye. Rejoice sis. You are **HIS!**

Marilyn's Short Sayings

Marilyn's Short Sayings

Some short phases that have helped me get through life:

1. Not every good thing is a God thing.

2. The right people will hear you. (credit Jason Gabhart)

3. It's okay to have the emotions. Just don't let the emotions have you.

4. Pray for your faith to be stronger and bigger than your feelings, flesh, and fear.

5. God saw you at your worst and still thought you were the best.

6. You can't receive unless you release.

7. Is it really the enemy or the inner me? (credit Jason Gabhart)

8. Sometimes, elevation requires separation.

9. You must let go of the old in order to walk into the new.

10. Don't let anyone rob you of your peace.

11. You don't have to answer to everything that calls your name.

12. Sometimes, you have to move in silence.

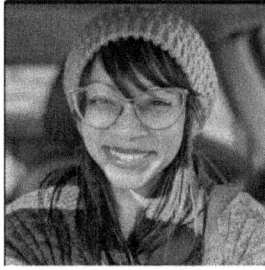

About the Author

Marilyn Majors is a born-again believer and disciple of Jesus Christ of Nazareth. When she isn't writing, you can find her watching black & white TV shows, older movies and classic TV series (TGIF). She enjoys the simple things in life such as nature walks, lounging on the beach, and museums. She is a full-time mom and risk adjustment coder with roots in KY.

This is Marilyn's fourth year of hosting Daughters of Zion. She also enjoys organizing as well as hosting women's conferences in hopes of seeing women of all ages come together for fellowship regardless of denomination, social status, and worldly differences. She is an encourager who brings hope, peace, and love as well as reminding ladies who they are in Christ.

If you would like to partner with Marilyn for an upcoming event or conference, you may contact her via Facebook at Marilyn Majors or send an email to
mari24savedbygrace@yahoo.com

Additional books by Marilyn:

"Echoes of His Love"

www.ingramcontent.com/pod-product-compliance
Lightning Source LLC
Chambersburg PA
CBHW051826090426
42736CB00011B/1673